TRANSGENDER
Journeys

TRANSGENDER Journeys

VIRGINIA RAMEY MOLLENKOTT
and VANESSA SHERIDAN

THE
PILGRIM
PRESS
Cleveland

The Pilgrim Press
700 Prospect Avenue
Cleveland, Ohio 44115-1100
pilgrimpress.com

Printed in the United States of America on acid-free paper

08   07   06   05   04   03   5   4   3   2   1

Library of Congress Cataloging-in-Publication Data

Mollenkott, Virginia R.
    Transgender journeys / Virginia Ramey Mollenkott and Vanessa
Sheridan.
        p.   cm.
    Includes bibliographical references (p.).
    ISBN 0-8298-1577-5 (pbk. : alk. paper)
    1. Transsexualism – Religious aspects – Christianity. 2. Christian
transsexuals – Religious life.   I. Sheridan, Vanessa, 1949-   II. Title.
BR115.T76 M655 2003
261.8′35768 – dc22

                                                            2003061325

*...the moment one definitely commits oneself,
then Providence moves too.*

—Johann Wolfgang von Goethe

CONTENTS

Introduction

WELCOME TO
THIS EXPLORATION!

I too am not a bit tamed.
I too am untranslatable.
I sound my barbaric yawp over the roofs of the world.
— Walt Whitman, *Leaves of Grass*

PERHAPS, LIKE WHITMAN, you feel yourself to be something of an untamed, untranslatable barbarian, fervently trumpeting your yawp over the world's rooftops. Or maybe you're quiet and shy, possibly embarrassed, perhaps even ashamed about having feelings of gender difference, especially in the light of your Christian beliefs. You may be unsure of what to do about that gender-related ambivalence, but deep down inside there's a gnawing sense that just maybe things could be better. Possibly you're questioning your gender orientation or that of someone you love, firmly convinced that gender-variant expression is incompatible with Christian spirituality.

Or perhaps you're a "straight" Christian who seeks accurate information, one who simply wants to do the right thing for gender-variant people in the Christian church. Maybe you're a clergyperson or a lay leader who'd like to make a difference for transgender[1] people in your congregation. No matter how you identify yourself on the wide spectrum of gender — and some people find themselves in significantly different locations on that spectrum from day to day — if you're Christian and if you care about issues of gender, transgender, and justice, this book is for you.

1

This book is about hope, opportunity, struggle, joy, difficulty, and transcendence. It is about God's abiding love for the remarkable created diversity of humankind. These pages offer information and inspiration while sharing real-life experiences about being both Christian and gender-variant. In addition, we wish to challenge and correct current falsification and abusive uses of the Bible against transgender Christians (and other "different" persons) who do not fit in to the demands of right-wing extremist religion. Our hope is to encourage readers by sparking ideas that can lead to positive actions which will make a liberating difference for society, for transgender Christians, and for the institutional Christian church. Our focus is on the sharing of the good news of God's love for all people, and our goal in writing this book is to increase awareness of the wonderful, edifying possibilities that await transgender Christians and the Christian church.

Just as we emerge from our mothers' wombs in a naked and vulnerable state, any authentic Christian journey must also begin with total honesty toward God, oneself, and others. A full frontal faith (or "spiritual nakedness," as we informally refer to it) is all about an unwavering spiritual commitment to becoming who we *really* are in all our relationships. It's about living in truth without sham or pretense, which is especially relevant for Christian transgender persons. A full frontal faith doesn't lend itself to spiritual deceit, trickery, or the manipulation of others, but instead motivates us to lead lives of integrity as the unique human beings we were created to be. A full frontal faith gently nudges us ever forward to be indwelt by the spirit of God, a spirit that urges us to draw a circle of loving relationship big enough to encompass even those who hate and judge us.

People who live out a full frontal faith are courageous enough both to bear and to bare the truth of what God is doing in and through them. They live unashamedly, with purpose, walking in the light of God's presence and strengthened by God's loving, relational spirit dwelling within them. A full frontal faith is both a challenge and a calling. It's a challenge because society isn't used to seeing courage, honesty, or openness in the lives of transgender Christians, and it's a calling because God's remarkable invitation to gender-variant Christians is to be mirrors of truth and hope as well as beacons of light and love in our hurting world.

We know that many Christians, both transgender and nontransgender, care deeply about justice and respect for all of humankind. These people seek to live in peace, harmony, mutuality, reciprocity, and right relationship with their fellow human beings. This book is for that often silent yet steadily growing group of people: those who may be disenchanted with "business as usual" in the church and society, those who seek information and encouragement in their struggles, those who have perhaps been disenfranchised by their religion or their faith communities, and those who would like to become part of an effort for positive change by creating justice.

Working for justice, especially within monolithic institutions like certain Christian churches, is a bit like cross-dressing. Some people think you're barking mad. But we who engage in it usually find the activity profoundly satisfying and rewarding. We discover a wholeness to life when we live out our values and embrace the reality of the gender-variant experience. We feel solid and grounded as we act with compassion for the oppressed and disenfranchised members of God's human family. Our simple prayer is that this book inspires and motivates you to join the growing movement to create justice for transgender persons within the church and society.

As we view it, our job as writers is to both inform and challenge you, the reader. Even as you read these words, we are already establishing a literary partnership of sorts, one in which, paradoxically, you are ultimately as responsible for the outcome as we. All parties in this unique, collaborative relationship are accountable for the end result: the writers must share their feelings, thoughts, and information with integrity, while readers must then determine how to accept, reject, discard, or apply those ideas within the context of their own lives. We thank The Pilgrim Press for its courageous commitment to gender justice, and Ulrike Guthrie for her expert editorial assistance.

Our hope is that all who read this book will become better informed, feel invited to explore new realities and truths, be challenged

to reevaluate their beliefs, and become increasingly aware of the necessity for doing justice work on behalf of transgender persons within
the institutional Christian church. Equipped with this awareness, may
we all work passionately and unceasingly to identify and change what
must be changed here in the real world, always doing the best we
can for the sake of the good and universally inclusive news of the
gospel.[2]

Chapter 1

EQUIPPING FOR
THE JOURNEY

IN THESE PAGES we want to share news and information about hope, promise, danger, difficulty, change, social and spiritual freedom, justice, grace, and God's transforming love for all people who would receive it. God is active and alive in our world and in our hearts, warming and tantalizing us with divine intimations of an astounding destiny for the human family. Let us pray that this sacred destiny is revealed to us as events continue to unfold. Let us also become proactive, cocreative partners with our creator in bringing this as-yet-unwritten human destiny to life.

We promise to you that we do not intentionally distort reality for the sake of making our argument(s), nor do we purposely attack any individual created in the image of God. However, we reserve the right to take issue with any unjust, antihuman group, organization, or ideology that may warp the inclusive, loving, accepting message of the One who energizes humankind and calls us toward reconciliation and healing. We ask only one thing of you: whether you agree or disagree with our statements and ideas, please read this book with an open heart and mind, allowing God's Holy Spirit to work within and through you. The results will surely be helpful in ways that neither you nor we can yet imagine.

The Christian church was established to enact, symbolize, and sustain the work of God on this earth. As Christians — the sisters and brothers of Jesus, the Christ — we are personally involved and invested in that work through prayer, doing good works, creating justice, developing right relationships, and making peace with all people everywhere. If this is true, and we are convinced it is, then the scope of those prayers, good works, justice efforts, right relationships, and peacemaking endeavors must also be extended to include God's beloved transgender persons, a greatly misunderstood, marginalized, and oppressed minority group within the church and society.

Our intention is certainly not to idealize or romanticize trans-genderists in these pages. To do so would be foolish, unfair, counter-productive, and inaccurate. Like any other demographic group in our society, the gender-variant community contains people who are paragons of virtue as well as people who have fallen through the cracks. Most of us, though, seem to reside somewhere in the middle. We're well aware that some transgender individuals present them-selves in an unattractive and sometimes ridiculously sensationalistic manner, often creating a significant public relations problem for the rest of us who are gender-variant and desire to live quiet, pro-ductive lives. We know that some transgender people engage in self-destructive or criminal activities that harm themselves and society in various ways. We are also aware, however, that most gender-variant persons are caring, generous, compassionate, loving people whose lives and work make profound contributions to the world. We transgenderists are everywhere, in every walk of life; and despite our transgender orientation, we are much more like everyone else than we aren't. In short, we are *people* — and therefore we deserve the same human, civil, and legal rights as any other citizen.

Because we are people, because we are human beings, because we are citizens, and because our transgender status places us at an un-deserved yet highly distinctive socioreligious disadvantage, "we must create a world of gender awareness — absolutely essential to self-awareness and to treating other people with equality, justice, and understanding — but we must not stop there."[1] Our lives and wit-ness clarify the fact that conventional definitions of "normal" often fail to encompass the personal, lived experiences of a considerable portion of humankind. Tucker Lieberman, an online commentator concerning gender and spirituality, offers this insight:

> "Gender" is only an open door to beginning to understand life. Gender, forgetting contemporary cultural specifications, is

ultimately the way that you manifest your life. Gender is not the duality of adult social prisons, not the simplicity of childhood ethics, not a simple-minded, dim justification for "keeping people in their proper place." Gender as [we are] using the word is the original sense of a "kind" or a "type." [We] mean the kind of person who you are, the kind of consciousness that you are, and most importantly the kind of person who you *want* and *choose* to be. Your gender is not prototyped in a static formation like a crystal; it is a process or a path.[2]

That journey of gender — the path of manifestation, consciousness, desire, and choice — can lead us to some astonishingly interesting places and experiences.

As cross-dressing college professor Michael "Miqqui Alicia" Gilbert has written:

Gender, certainly in our culture, is emphatically bipolar. That is, there are two socially identified genders, men and women, and each individual within the society is expected to fall neatly into one of those two categories. Of course, not everyone does, and those who do not [must] pay the price through such various mechanisms of social control as ridicule, ostracism, systemic discrimination, legal and social persecution, medical mutilation, institutional isolation, state supported harassment, and even death. The bipolar gender system is not only a cultural phenomenon supported by a multitude of societal mores, customs and institutions. It is also a highly policed legal institution as well.[3]

Ray Charles, the American musical treasure, has said, "Music always reflects the culture, and is often ahead of its time." What is true for music is also true for transgender individuals: gender-variant persons are society's mirrors, reflecting and often helping to precipitate change in the culture's gender-based expectations and social mores. We are pioneers who demonstrate and embody elements of what is possible for human beings as we journey to and then beyond the frontiers of traditional gendering.

Julie Ann Johnson writes, "Being a Christian and also being a cross-dresser or a transsexual is not an unusual phenomenon. In fact, there are large numbers of transgender people who profess their faith in Jesus Christ. Unfortunately, and too often, when a transgender person is found out by members of their church, there is movement to ostracize them."[4] Becky Allison adds, "There seems to be no shortage of persons who would tell us everything we are doing wrong in our lives. Some of the most self-assured are those who claim to know the will of God for other persons."[5] It seems there are always people in the church who would substitute a pseudoreligious state of enforced conformity for the experience of compassionate, spirit-filled actions and behaviors. Any quarrel we may have is not with our Christian sisters and brothers, but with an oppressive religious ideology that insists upon loving and vilifying transgender persons at the same time. Like newspaper columnist Kim Ode, we contend that the old "love the sinner, hate the sin" philosophy "always sounds quite noble, though it only seems to get invoked when someone wants to sound compassionate despite holding an uncompassionate viewpoint."[6]

CRITICAL ELEMENTS AND TRANSGENDER YOUTH

Rather than futilely attempting to change the God-given identities of gender-variant people, perhaps we Christians would do better to work toward transforming and eliminating our society's institutionalized attitudes of exclusivity, bigotry, homophobia, and transphobia. An esteemed cross-dressing Christian sociologist, Pat Conover, has written,

> Individually and collectively, we face the human task of making sense of the facets of reality that we know through our senses. Although the idea of gender seems fixed and simple to many people, [persons of conscience must strongly consider] the complexity, flexibility, and interactivity of physiological and psychological factors that affect the creation, transmission, and changing of gender categories and images.[7]

Frankly, paying attention to gender complexities is the only just and reasonable thing to do.

Toward that end, we believe that the religious, medical, and psychological communities must stop pathologizing us and begin respecting the inherent complexity of transgender experience. As Conover's extensive analysis demonstrates, much of the cultural negativity that currently exists results from misuse, misunderstandings, or misinterpretations of scientific and psychological data regarding transgenderism. Those unfortunate circumstances have often led to an undeserved and debilitating pathological diagnosis for gender-variant persons. Conover puts the problem in perspective when she says,

> It is not scientifically reasonable for psychologists and psychiatrists to pathologize transgender behavior by saying the equivalent of "Oh, that must be because of some brain, or other physiological, defect." It is far more reasonable to argue that complex, flexible, interactive brains give rise to complex, flexible, interactive mental constructs, which are melded together in complex, flexible, and interactive social and cultural activities to create observable, complex, flexible, and interactive gender [expression and gender] roles.[8]

In fact, one online commentator has described the attitudes of those pathologizing communities as "the toxic ... oppression of the psycho-medicalizing discourse that makes everyday transgender experiences fit into a disease model of gender identity disorder, body dysphoria, social deviancy, and personal deficiency."[9]

Perhaps most important of all, the church and society's institutions must begin recognizing and working to dispel the pervasive, culturally induced despair and emotional/spiritual anguish that afflict so many of our gender- and sex-variant young people. Gilbert writes,

> Consider ... the young transgendered person, [perhaps] a little boy who in watching the world around him in whole or in part identifies with little girls as much as or more than [with] little boys. That is, at least some of the time, this little boy wants to

be or wishes he was or was more like the little girls he sees. . . . It is usually at the onset of puberty when things will come to a head. In other words, the young gender outlaw is at that threshold when, more and more, the distinction between the genders widens and the separate societal identified paths must be taken. What happens to this young boy? Well, he learns very quickly not to make these desires public. His play habits and mannerisms are watched and corrected if he violates the gender laws. He learns to sublimate the feelings of wrong-ness. . . . [10]

What is true for young boys is also true for young girls, as you will read in Virginia's account of her gender journey.

Those socially derived feelings of wrongness often manifest themselves in harmful, even deadly ways. Gianna Israel writes, "Youth who are continually forced to comply with social stereotypes may develop behavioral problems or depression. Like adult transgender persons, they may also become estranged from family relationships. Youth who become disillusioned with their families may end up homeless and at risk of victimization and disease. Some may commit suicide, leaving others with no explanation or insight into the pain they were suffering."[11]

Psychologist Paul Cody tells us that only in the last decade has there been recognition that gay, lesbian, bisexual, and transgender youth (generally defined as ages fifteen to twenty-four) are at a greatly increased risk of suicide in comparison to non-GLBT youth. Research literature provides estimates that gay, lesbian, and bisexual youth attempt suicide at a rate some two or three times higher than their heterosexual peers. A few studies have indicated that the rate of attempted suicide for transgender youth is more than 50 percent. There are also estimates that gay, lesbian, and bisexual youth constitute 30 percent of all completed suicides, with transgender youth also having an extremely high incidence of completed suicides.[12]

Cody goes on to say that a lethal combination of societal and developmental factors creates this greatly increased risk of suicide for sexual- and gender-minority youth. These young people are at an age period when everyone faces the developmental tasks of finding a personal identity and learning about sexual/emotional intimacy in relationships. Heterosexual and nontransgender youth are fostered, nurtured, and channeled in these endeavors. In fact, heterosexual and nontransgender youth have their feelings, identities, and relationships acknowledged and validated, both implicitly and explicitly, by an encouraging society. Generally speaking, though, our society is a harsh and difficult environment for sexual- and gender-minority youth, because the resources that might help those young people in their development are absent in most places, and insufficient in others. It is difficult for these youth because they must try to steer around specific hazards to their emotional and physical health. Sexual- and gender-minority youth are the frequent targets of harassment, threats of violence, and physical/sexual assaults by peers and even family. Slurs, insults, and jokes directed toward these young people pervade their environment and create a major challenge for them to find ways to love themselves and develop healthy self-esteem. Sadly, many of these youth do not possess the internal and external resources nor the self-sufficiency that comes with age to assist them in their struggles. Consequently, they internalize self-hatred and inner pain, often resulting in a higher risk of alcohol and drug abuse as a way to numb those feelings of inadequacy and shame.[13]

Cody's assessments are borne out by our firsthand experience and observations. Virginia well remembers her own experiences as a transgender teenager. When her mother discovered that Virginia was in a lesbian relationship, she sent her to a Southern Presbyterian high school in Florida. Before her arrival the administration told the entire student body that she was dangerous and must never be alone with anyone. Periodically administrators told her that although there was no cure for her disease, nevertheless God had no use for her kind of person. After several months of such abuse, she tried to comply with the message she was receiving by attempting to kill herself. Years later, Virginia's son Paul helped her realize the full horror of what had been taught to her. Hearing his mother mention on a television show that she'd been convinced God did not love her, Paul became so shocked that Virginia at last realized that those administrators had inflicted hideous injury upon "one of these little ones" that

Jesus loved. Alas, her story is more typical than many of us would like to believe.

Sex- and gender-variant young people are hurting, and many of them are dying because we (adults, parents, friends, the church, society) aren't doing anything to help them. Their pain and confusion often manifests itself either in various self-destructive behaviors or in suicide. Ignoring or minimizing the problem of such emotional pain is inexcusable and unacceptable, especially for people who call themselves Christians, followers of the compassionate Jesus. Recognizing this issue is especially important if you are the parent of a transgender young person because — believe us — your child didn't choose to be gender-variant. For the sake of your transgender son or daughter, please don't let him/her continue to live in turmoil, despair, and fear if you can do something about it. Young people don't need condemnation or rejection, but they desperately need our love. We must do all we can to reach out in compassion and acceptance, and we cannot put it off until tomorrow; we must begin now, today. Literally, lives are at stake.

BECOMING AGENTS OF CHANGE

Becoming visible and vocal within the staid, change-resistant corridors of institutional Christianity poses, of course, a tremendous challenge on many fronts. The Reverend Dr. Christine M. Smith writes, "Dismantling oppressive theological constructs is as painful as proclaiming redemptive activity and liberation is celebrative. Both are needed."[14] We — as individuals, as communities of faith, and as a universal church — must first experience the pain of *de*constructing oppressive theologies before we can move forward into the celebration of liberative, redemptive theological *con*struction founded upon the values of justice, respect, and mutuality. But it is always much simpler to deconstruct or dismantle something than to develop a workable plan for constructing or building anything new. That's why we must keep clinging to the hope that Jesus exemplified for us, the hope that after the pain of deconstruction and death will come the joy of reconstruction and new life. We should keep in mind that while we can't control the wind, we can always adjust our sails. Continuous theological and attitudinal reconstruction is not only possible but essential.

This book is intended to highlight the need for healing and reconciliation by encouraging the active, dynamic development of a new and enriched spiritual environment within our faith communities. Such an environment must be inclusive, respectful, and welcoming to every person — young or old; black, white, red, brown, or yellow; of all economic and social strata; of every age and physical/mental status; straight, gay, lesbian, bisexual, or transgender — all of whom are created in love and for love by a God who embraces and blesses the astonishing diversity within the human family.

Please be aware, however, that our journey-by-book is not intended to be a comprehensive, in-depth explanation or summation of the complex issues — histories, etiological factors, varied orientations, physical and emotional manifestations, and so forth — relevant to the social constructs of gender, gender roles, and gender expectations. Those topics are covered quite well and more extensively in other works, and we encourage you to seek out books and articles that address with integrity and accurate scholarship these particular issues.[15] The list of published scholarly works that speak to transgender-related concerns continues to grow, and we are grateful for that although much work remains to be done in terms of understanding gender variance on a cultural level.

We ourselves have provided two such books, the books through which we met one another, began a correspondence, developed a friendship, and decided to write together: Virginia Ramey Mollenkott's *Omnigender: A Trans-Religious Approach,* and Vanessa Sheridan's *Crossing Over: Liberating the Transgender Christian,* both published in 2001 by The Pilgrim Press of Cleveland, Ohio. Virginia's book surveys the status of transgender people in a variety of cultures and religions, and suggests moving away from the inaccurate binary gender paradigm toward a sex/gender continuum that would honor God's presence in all people of every gender identity. Vanessa's book focuses on the experience of transgender Christians, the need for their full inclusion into the life and ministry of the Christian church, and the need for developing a transgender-based theology of liberation. *Transgender Journeys* is a cooperative attempt to contribute to that theological development and understanding.

As for the religious right of which transgender Christians must be aware, excellent studies are available. We especially admire Bruce Bawer's *Stealing Jesus: How Fundamentalism Betrays Christianity* (New York: Crown, 1997), and Carter Heyward's *Saving Jesus from Those Who Are Right: Rethinking What It Means to Be Christian* (Minneapolis: Augsburg Fortress, 1999). Our intention in this book is to develop more fully what those books touch upon tangentially: the relationship between Christian theologies and the specifically transgender people in the church. We want to encourage thinking about these issues, believing that from such thought will emerge new ideas and subsequent opportunities for creating positive change.

SEEKING CLARITY OF VISION

Taking a cue from Viktor E. Frankl's inspirational work, *Man's Search for Meaning,* we view our role as "that of an eye specialist rather than that of a painter."[16] Frankl tells us that painters try to convey a picture of the world as they see it, while ophthalmologists try to help us see the world as it really is. Jesus Seminar scholar Marcus J. Borg says, "A worldview is one's most basic image of 'what is' — of what is real and what is possible.... A religious worldview sees reality as grounded in the sacred."[17] Though from our perspective the religious right continually makes feverish attempts to obfuscate clarity and refute progressive insights while imposing their own version of "truth" upon everyone else, we can only hope that many of us become willing to try to see the remarkable diversity of creation as it is constituted.

This is why, like Christine Smith, we must "seek to shape theology and the practice of ministry in response to the concrete realities of human suffering and oppression and toward a vision of liberation and restoration."[18] A basic rule for faith and theology is that both must be lived out here in the real world if they are to mean anything. We must discover the impetus for our actions "emerging from the larger social context of our individual and collective lives."[19] If you are more interested in learning about the real lives, current social contexts, and legitimate spiritual concerns of transgender Christians than you are in continuing to reinforce any perhaps unfounded prejudices toward the gender-variant, then we welcome your company on what will surely prove to be a fascinating journey of exploration and discovery. Let's get packing!

Chapter 2

REORDERING OUR
TRAVEL PRIORITIES

☿ IN THIS CHAPTER we explore some of the mental and emotional gear that must be repacked and rearranged in order to accommodate major changes in a belief system that may previously have been unquestioned. What happens, for instance, when we suddenly find ourselves confronted by a person who doesn't fit into a predetermined, socially acceptable, "normal" gender cubbyhole? (Because various cultures differ about what is acceptable, we recognize and apply any definition of "normal" solely as a statistical average, not as a value judgment.) How do we deal with a person whose gender presentation or expression might not be congruent with our expectations? How do we cope with someone who has a "different" gender orientation? How do we handle the unfamiliarity, the feelings of uncertainty and ambiguity that the mere presence of such a person might evoke? What should we do when we're confronted with people whose life and personal manner of gender expression are simply outside our current frame of reference? Do we ignore them, reject them, vilify and demonize them, or do we welcome their presence, learn from them, recognize their gifts, affirm their humanity, and embrace them as sisters or brothers in God's family? The answers to these questions directly influence our attitudes and actions toward those who are "other." As we live into the answers, we must keep in mind that Christians have a God-given mandate to welcome and embrace the stranger by continually demonstrating hospitality to those who stand in need of it. We aren't necessarily expected to understand or know everything about other people: we're told to love them.

The book of Ecclesiastes reminds us that all is vanity (Eccles. 1:2) and that our brief existence is little more than a breath of time in God's eternity. Nevertheless, what we do on this earth during our short sojourn counts for a great deal. What lives on after us is the love we leave behind; anything of lasting value that we ultimately produce will consist of the positive differences we have made in the lives of others, and those they have made in ours. That will be our eternal legacy as human beings who, together with God and all other creatures, are partners in a magnificent cosmic dance.

Our very nature is to want specific answers to questions about the meaning of life. That is, after all, why religion was invented in the first place. Mythologist Joseph Campbell has said, "Life has no meaning. You bring meaning to life." Each of us creates meaning and context for our existence through ideas, values, interests, passions, behaviors, choices, intentions, attitudes, and actions. Philosopher and social critic John W. Gardner has written, "Meaning is something you build into your own life. You build it out of your own past, out of your affections and loyalties, out of the experience of humankind as it is passed on to you, out of your own talent and understanding, out of the things you believe in, out of the things and people you love, out of the values for which you are willing to sacrifice something."[1] So when we are confronted with unexpected aspects of ourselves or others, we are building our own life's meaning by the way we respond.

Many of us, though, still cling to the oh-so-human and perhaps rather idealistic notion that we need immutable rules and unmistakably clear parameters that can be easily applied to every situation. We like to be able to figure out everything in advance, and we want to do it according to our personal paradigms and comfort levels. We desperately wish to meet life on our own terms and in the light of our personal assumptions, thus artificially controlling our circumstances so we can know how we should think and feel at all times. That way we won't have to constantly assess and question everything. We don't want our orthodoxies challenged; it's too much work to think about all these things at every moment.

Many of us live in fear of change because change represents the unknown, and we flinch before what we don't know or understand.

In addition, a good many of us "resist that which is confusing, and cherish that which is simple. [We] want to push a button and watch it work."[2] The fact that many of us crave simplicity, and reject ambiguity or complexity, explains why religious fundamentalism appears so attractive to some; we don't have to think very hard, stay continually vigilant and aware, or grow in our acceptance and respect for life's mysteries if we're immersed in a closed, black-and-white belief system — a spiritual ghetto, so to speak — that ostensibly supplies all we need to know (or all that religious authorities want us to know) about life's questions.

Virginia has never forgotten a moment about thirty years ago when one of her state college students told her that he was starting his transition from male to female. Suddenly Virginia felt as if the chair under her had squirmed, as if the very floor of the office were shifting under her feet. Simultaneously she felt honored that he had trusted her with this information, and she attempted to provide loving support. Not until she had researched and written *Omnigender* did she understand why her sensations at that time were so extreme. Cultural beliefs about gender run very deep, and for the first time she was conscious of encountering a human being whose experience proved that her assumptions were not accurate. Later she would also realize that her own life experience had always been proving the same thing. But when it comes to understanding ourselves, it is often a case of "too soon old, and too late smart!"

Vanessa, too, has come to recognize that her life's experiences are ongoing proof of the inaccuracy of her childhood assumptions about our culture's rigid, polarized system of gender. She intuitively knew at an early age that her own gender-based self-perception was at odds with the androcentric social expectations that she encountered and internalized. She learned to "fake it" quite well but, like Virginia, any actual cognitive/emotional/spiritual understanding of what was actually going on came about much later. Vanessa has learned that just as the factors which create transgenderism are interrelated, "the forces which contribute to transphobia [also] interweave, creating oppositions to diverse gender identification and expression."[3]

Jack Rogers, moderator of the 213th General Assembly of the Presbyterian Church (U.S.A.), describes an important discovery he made during his doctoral studies in theology: that there is a kind of conservatism that "confuses Christianity with our culture," a conservatism that substitutes a form of American folk religion for the principles of love and mutuality that Jesus taught and modeled so well. Although at the time he was himself a stringent conservative, Rogers discovered that "Salvation is not found in the status quo. From apostolic times Christians have challenged the existing [social] order."[4] Therefore, Rogers comments, "I feel no need to apologize for my past. Nor do I feel sorry that I am continually moving beyond it." (Would that we might all progress into the future with such spiritual equanimity and optimism!) He agrees with Pastor John Robinson, one of the original Pilgrims, that God always has "yet more light to break forth from [God's] word."[5]

Like Jack Rogers, we believe that God has not called us to live our lives within the confines of inflexible, antihuman ideologies; of narrow, unimaginative spiritual thinking; or of closed, exclusivist religious belief systems. Too many among us have been overwhelmed by judgmentalism in the name of religion instead of love in the name of relationship. We've watched in sorrow as religious perversion catapulted people like Osama bin Laden, suicide bombers, and other terrorists from many nations (all claiming to act "in the name of God") into the forefront of our global consciousness.

At the time of Jesus' physical presence upon this earth, the Samaritan was the symbol of bigotry and prejudice for all observant Jews. Samaritans were loathed, despised, rejected, and considered unworthy of even breathing the air. Today, for folks with a traditionalist mind-set, transgender persons (along with lesbians, gays, and bisexuals) are filling that same symbolic role. We are considered "untouchables" and undesirables within traditional Christianity. We are the socioreligious pariahs of the twenty-first century. We are the new Samaritans.

But here is the good news: the gospel of Jesus Christ challenges each one of us to move beyond the external differences that separate us as people. Jesus' loving, inclusive example calls us to a new way of being in relationship, a way of living without erecting artificial barriers of prejudice. Through the love of Christ it becomes possible for us to know the reality of a new kind of liberating relationship, one rooted in mutual respect and appreciation for our shared humanity — a humanity created in God's relational image.

We must acknowledge that a spirituality rooted in liberation is predicated upon the conviction that the systemically oppressive structure of society and its institutions is always open to reconstruction in the service of greater justice. In a specifically transgender-based theology of liberation (or in any other liberation theology, for that matter), proactively striving for positive social change is recognized as a necessary condition in order to foster liberation for everyone. Peacefully striving to eliminate oppression through positively transforming an unjust social structure is doing the work of creating justice.

Our goal must always be that of a comprehensive transformation: not only a personal transformation but a transformation of the culture and its institutions, including the Christian church, as part of the package of liberative justice. This implies the need for both an internal and an external transformation. As we've already stated, the inherent complexity of such transformations poses a challenge for us all. Personal and institutional transformation is not only possible but absolutely necessary if we are to create justice and right relationships between people.

Both types of transformation must be desired and pursued simultaneously because, like the web of injustices, they are inextricably connected. Therefore, we must focus our energies and attention on identifying, documenting, and actively confronting the root causes of the problems in our world — problems that reflect and perpetuate systemic oppression and injustice — if we are to foster liberation for transgender persons. Just as the world won't be rid of terrorism until lovelessness, poverty, hunger, homelessness, and economic instability are effectively overcome, transgender people will not be welcomed and respected in our churches until the pivotal issues of Christian lovelessness, bigotry, oppression, and fear of the other are confronted and transcended.

Christine Smith helps us gain a broader and more universal perspective on this issue when she writes,

> If sin is that which is done by the individual self, then engaging in individualized repentance and seeking personal forgiveness become the needed actions. If sin and evil are understood as having political, social, systemic roots and realities, then individual and collective conversion and organized resistance become the called for and necessary actions. It is never that individual repentance is unimportant; it simply is not enough to stop the social and political crucifixions that strip people of their humanity and their lives.[6]

Virginia came across a comment somewhere during the writing of this book that stopped her in her tracks: "It's much easier to be moral if you have some security somewhere in your life." She thought about all the poverty-stricken peasants who for centuries were hanged for stealing food to feed their hungry children, and realized how pathetic it is to feel self-righteous over observing property boundaries when one has secure boundaries of one's own — a home and a refrigerator full of food. On the other hand, it should be easier for Christians to support gender justice if we feel the security of knowing that God created gender diversity in the first place.

In an article on pastoral care, Kathleen D. Billman says that the task of organized resistance is "especially critical when survival is at stake, because when difference becomes too much of a threat there will be strong moves to silence voices that have criticized the status quo. Nearly every mainstream Protestant denomination in the United States is now experiencing a strong backlash against feminists, womanists, and other minority voices — male and female." She explains the various factors involved in this backlash: "resistance to the increased freedom of those who are claiming their right to speak and press for change"; "the pain and anger of lost privilege on the part of those who were always looked to for leadership in the past"; "the terror caused by massive social upheaval"; and finally, the mutual distrust between ecclesial academies and local congregants in identifying and exploring the roots of social upheaval.[7]

These varied dynamics create many complexities for us within society, in our churches, and certainly in our individual lives. Creating
liberative justice is a task that is far too great for one person to accomplish alone. It takes a committed community, working together
and uniting its talents, abilities, and strengths, to bring about the
desired and necessary changes. Such a task also demands an uncom-
promising willingness to confront and honestly analyze our beliefs,
and perhaps to change or even abandon those beliefs if they do not
reflect an unwavering commitment to justice for all people. That's
often an extremely difficult and courageous thing to do, especially in
the face of socioreligious pressures like those created by the religious
right, but it's necessary if we hope to live lives of Christlike integrity.
As Billman goes on to remind us, "For those who exist on the margins of established order, the upheaval in the 'center' is filled not only
with danger but with possibility as well."[8] May we learn to celebrate
our possibilities without letting down our guard against the dangers!

DISTINGUISHING EXTREMISM FROM SPIRITUAL BALANCE

Unfortunately, religious extremists usually have no time for honest
doubt, deep inquiry, or a healthy skepticism (i.e., a hermeneutic of
suspicion) with regard to issues of spiritual substance. Virginia remembers a professor of theology at her alma mater, fundamentalist
Bob Jones University, who habitually discouraged probing questions
by saying, "If it's not in the syllabus, it's not important." Vanessa
recalls an incident that occurred when she was around twelve or thirteen years old: she began questioning and ruminating openly on the
believability of some of the Bible stories she heard in Sunday school,
which soon prompted a home visit from her fundamentalist pastor.
She remembers being scared to death when the large man boomed,
"So what's this I hear about you not believing the Bible?" Almost
paralyzed by the thought of potential physical punishment from her
parents or of spiritual retribution from on high, she managed to apologize and mumble something about only being curious. To Vanessa's
vast relief, this bumbling strategy apparently managed to placate the
minister and defuse the incident.

A closed, highly conservative ideology fears anything that may smack of change, newness, modernism, or humanism. Fundamentalists tend to become the sirens of dogmatic orthodoxy, often approaching the future by retreating into the perceived security of a bygone era. (William Faulkner once wrote, "The past is not dead. It's not even past." For some, Faulkner's remark appears to be an unfortunately accurate description.) In particular, right-wing religious ideologues insist that change may introduce madness or chaos, and a good fundamentalist — steeped in a patriarchal, heterosexist, transphobic mind-set and tradition — simply can't permit *that*. Maintaining power and conformity over the ways people think and behave is a critical tool for those in power on the religious right.

Again, Bob Jones University provides an example of this attempt to ward off any and every possible change. When Virginia was a student there in the early 1950s, the founder and president, Dr. Bob Jones Sr., buried on the campus a time capsule containing a full description of the doctrines, rules, and regulations of the school. The capsule was designed to be dug up and opened fifty years later. If any doctrine, rule, policy, or regulation had been changed to the slightest degree, the university was to be closed and the campus bombed into extinction. (The time has come and gone, and despite important changes such as admitting African American students, no bombing has taken place. But the founder's intentions were clear nevertheless.)

Vanessa recently visited her mother in the southeastern United States, who warmly invited her to attend church services on Sunday morning. Though (by personal choice) Vanessa hadn't been inside a Southern Baptist church in nearly twenty-five years, her curiosity was aroused and she decided to go. Besides, Vanessa loves her mom dearly, and she knew that going to church would greatly please her mother. Entering the sanctuary, Vanessa was immediately transported back to the fundamentalist days of her youth: practically nothing had changed. Somehow everything felt, sounded, and even *smelled* the same, which was patently absurd since she had never been in this particular building before. In the immortal words of Yogi Berra, it was like *déjà vu* all over again. Still, Vanessa couldn't believe it — the hymns for the service were the same ones she'd memorized and sung all throughout her youth. She knew every verse and every line of every song. The order of service hadn't changed; the prayers, offering, congregational hymns, the biblical literalist preaching, the ubiquitous use of "thees" and "thous" in prayers, the all-male language for God — every element of the worship service was precisely as she remembered. Vanessa gritted her teeth and prayed the entire time. She felt as though she were in a time warp, almost if she might have somehow wandered into another dimension or a parallel universe of some sort.

Upon leaving the church, Vanessa silently gave thanks to God for having brought her out of such a spiritually stifling religious environment. To Vanessa's eyes, positive change, genuine spiritual enlightenment, and a progressive theological understanding did not appear to be important components of Southern Baptist culture. But she was glad she'd gone to visit on that hot Sunday morning, first because she verified the legitimacy of her own awareness about the spiritual damage she experienced during her fundamentalist youth; second, because she knew that, despite the differences in their theological perspectives, accompanying her mom to church had made her mother truly happy.

Noted theologians and scholars Martin E. Marty and R. Scott Appleby have argued that, whether the religion be Christianity, Judaism, or Islam, "the 'fundamentalisms' all follow a certain pattern. They are embattled forms of spirituality, which have emerged as a response to a perceived crisis. . . . [Fundamentalists] fear annihilation, and try to fortify their beleaguered identity by means of a selective retrieval of certain doctrines and practices of the past."[9]

Author Karen Armstrong adds, "Fundamentalists feel that they are battling against forces that threaten their most sacred values. During a war it is very difficult for combatants to appreciate one another's position."[10] Make no mistake: as least as far as the extreme religious right is concerned, they are engaged in a holy war, a *jihad* of their own, against the perceived threat posed by the encroaching forces of modernism in the form of socioreligious change. One can perhaps respect their sense of loyalty to their values, but it's exceedingly difficult for any thinking, compassionate Christian to admire the values of exclusion, religious paranoia, prejudice, and hatred of anyone who dares to disagree. Too often these values form the content of a fundamentalist worldview.

Religious fundamentalism tends to shrink God into a more "manageable," anthropomorphized, and, always, male-oriented perspective. Slotting God into the sociopolitical agenda and accompanying rhetoric of exclusivist ideologies then becomes possible. Fundamentalists work diligently to make our intricate modern world appear more simple and comfortable for people who are confused or fearful, and that religious illusion in turn offers an apparent but false sense of both mission and security. This illusion of religious security has often been an excellent tool for swelling the ranks of fundamentalist churches. Naturally, such an ethos must avoid addressing theological complexities and spiritual ambiguities, adhering instead to a rigid, black-and-white version of religious "truth," a skewed perspective on reality that is loudly declared to be universal and thus inarguable and unassailable.

Not surprisingly, along the way some people develop the notion that clinging tightly to their belief system is somehow more important than the real lives of real people living in the real world with real problems and real spiritual concerns. A simplistic, fear-based fundamentalist worldview cannot effectively address legitimate human problems or concerns because it lacks the necessary inclusive and compassionate depth, spiritual perspective, and substance to do so. Instead of expanding one's awareness, embracing mystery and wonder, and enriching one's existence, such a limiting ideology actually shrinks a person's life. Conversely, opening up to a new reality enriches life. The organization known as PFLAG (Parents and Friends of Lesbians and Gays, which has opened its arms to bisexuals and transgenderists as well) is full of folks with wonderful, heartwarming stories about how every family member benefited from stretching to embrace their member who was "different." And all of us owe ourselves at least one trip to observe the Special Olympics. Virginia's first visit was inspired by the desire to be helpful, but it was the "special" athletes and observers who showed her such utterly unconditional love and boundless egalitarian acceptance that she has never forgotten the sensation. "Special" indeed!

It's always a shame when the rules of an organization supersede and become more important than the people they were designed to help. Jesus understood this principle perfectly. He gave us a wonderful framework for assessing such matters when he simply and profoundly taught, "The sabbath was made for humankind, and not humankind for the sabbath" (Mark 2:27). Jesus knew that the souls of people were always infinitely more important than any religious rules, structures, or traditions. Jesus didn't want to eradicate religion, but he wanted us to understand that real, life-changing religion is, in the end, always about people, not regulations. Jesus said he didn't come to abolish the law, but to fulfill it (Matt. 5:17) — which means that, through Jesus' message of universal love and salvation, the law is magnificently transformed into something that liberates people instead of oppressing them. That's a far cry from the rigid, unjust, and exclusivist ideologies of contemporary fundamentalism.

RESPECTING THE REALITIES OF GOD'S CREATION

Armstrong tells us that fundamentalism also attempts to turn spiritually rich Christian myths[11] into scientific facts, creating a hybrid that is neither good science nor good religion. This runs counter to the whole history of spirituality because, by definition, religious truth is not naturalistic and cannot be proved scientifically.[12] Armstrong writes, "By insisting that the truths of Christianity are factual and scientifically demonstrable, American Protestant fundamentalists have created a caricature of both religion and science."[13] We might well remember that statement the next time some religious right-winger asserts that living one's life as a gender-variant individual is tantamount to insulting the laws of God and nature. Such an assertion is not only bad theology but bad science as well.

Christian ethicist Christine E. Gudorf recently issued a challenge to the church in the *Journal of the American Academy of Religion*.[14] Citing the accumulation of biological, psychological, sociological, and anthropological evidence that human beings are not neatly divided into airtight male and female categories, but rather live their lives somewhere along a sex/gender continuum, Gudorf explains that the evidence is now great enough to call the dimorphic (male vs. female) gender/sex paradigm into serious question. She warns that the church must begin to make an appropriate response to this compelling evidence if it wishes to exert any meaningful influence on the paradigm shift currently in progress. Virginia's book *Omnigender* goes into great detail concerning the sex/gender continuum as evidenced in the lives of intersexuals, transsexuals, homosexuals, bisexuals, crossdressers, other transgenderists, and heterosexuals who do not or cannot conform to society's gender role expectations.

What happens in the human species is reflected also in the remainder of creation, as biologist Bruce Bagemihl clarifies in his study entitled *Biological Exuberance: Animal Homosexuality and the Natural Diversity* (New York: St. Martin's Press, 1999). *Kirkus Reviews* describes Bagemihl's evidence as "meticulously gathered," "cogently delivered," and "utterly convincing." The evidence proves that human homosexuality and transgenderism are not aberrations in nature, but are reflected everywhere in a creation that is both polysexual and polygendered. Anyone who has believed the statement that only human beings are depraved enough to be homosexual, intersexual, or otherwise transgender should take the time to examine Bagemihl's 751 pages packed with powerful evidence to the contrary.

Once a person has seen and begun to comprehend the fact that life is inherently messy and interdependent, that no one religion or belief system neatly holds all the answers, and that some aspects of life must simply be accepted and pondered rather than smoothly explained away, that person is no longer able to turn a blind eye and a deaf ear to matters of injustice and oppression. No longer can we accept anyone's insistence that his or her methods alone hold the key to how everyone else should think, believe, and behave. Nor can we imagine that we ourselves are absolutely correct and innocent. A subtle yet fundamental shift occurs in the way we perceive the world and our place in it, and we can never completely go back to the way things used to be. In the sense of spiritual awakening, at least, Thomas Wolfe was correct: We can't go home again. We may refer to this type of dawning awareness by various names: the death of innocence, disillusionment, a loss of naïveté, the acceptance of vulnerability, or the recognition of our own inevitable complicity in evils such as racism and economic exploitation. Some just call it growing up.

IMAGERY CONCERNING GOD AND SPIRITUAL MATURITY

Vanessa writes:

Speaking of growing up, I'd like to begin promoting the religiously unorthodox idea that we Christians might do well to begin moving away from our traditional understanding of God as a doting heavenly parent. That parental image seems to portray God as someone who has a pathological need to watch over us and take care of us at every moment of our entire lives. It implies that we are helpless and unable to do anything of significance on our own behalf.

I'm certainly not saying that we should all turn our backs on the deity or that we should sever our connection with our creator. What I am suggesting is that God might possibly prefer to have each of us reach a point of maturation in our faith and in our awareness of who and what we are so that we might actually begin figuring some things out for ourselves, at least to whatever degree is possible for us.

I believe God might like you and me to demonstrate a little growth, a little chutzpah, a little interest in thinking and behaving like grown-ups, and perhaps a little less passive dependency. Maybe God is even growing a bit tired of being "our Father [or Mother] in heaven," with all the attendant parental responsibilities that such a title implies. Perhaps God would prefer to see us achieve a spiritual coming-of-age by adopting a bit of accountability for making our own decisions and acting like people who have minds and wills of our own. After all, God was the one who ostensibly gave us those qualities in the first place; is it possible that God would actually expect us to use them responsibly?

A total lifelong dependence on the deity for being overly concerned with our every little need, no matter how minute, seems somehow antithetical to the concept of a growing, dynamic, and mature Christianity. Besides, whatever happened to the idea that "God helps those who help themselves"? We would seemingly perform a service for all concerned by learning how to do as much for ourselves as possible instead of continuing to rely solely on the whims and benevolent parental nature of our creator to safeguard and oversee every small aspect of our existence. After all, an important mark of adulthood is moving out from under the wing of one's parents and assuming responsibility for one's own choices. Why should our lives of faith be any different? Why shouldn't we strive to reach at least some semblance of spiritual adulthood in terms of our relationships with God and each other?

Realistically, I don't expect masses of people to actively embrace this idea. It depends too much on the expectations of personal accountability and individual initiative, plus it actually requires one to begin thinking and doing for oneself. Some of us don't appear to welcome these activities with any great degree of enthusiasm, especially when it comes to matters of spiritual significance. To be frank, many of us are mentally and spiritually lazy. As Henry Ford once said, "Thinking is the hardest work there is, which is why so few people engage in it." It's so much easier to let God or God's designated representatives take care of us and tell us what to do and how to do it instead of thinking for ourselves and actually doing the work, isn't it?

Virginia responds:

Vanessa's ponderings about moving beyond parental images of God have a good deal of biblical support. Most notable perhaps is Ephesians 4:14–15: "We must no longer be children.... But ... we must grow up in every way into the One who is the head, into Christ." Not only does this urging give the lie to the notion that the head/body imagery of Ephesians 5 is intended to teach female subordination to male leadership; it also teaches that Jesus is not so much to be worshiped as to be emulated and embodied in mature Christian lives.

FINDING OUR VOICE

Assuming that we are willing to take the spiritual journey together and that we are truly endeavoring to grow up into the Christ, we are increasingly confronted by the questionable ethics of the larger culture and its institutions, and we Christians are certainly not immune to the detrimental effects of this social malaise. We often find that we are more concerned with being "right" and appearing to have it all together than with being faithful to God's holy calling to live our lives with as much integrity as we can muster. Transgender folks are no different in this regard; we're human too, with the combination of relational power and vulnerability that being human entails. Heaven knows we make our fair share of mistakes. However, as gender-variant people we have also been and continue to be the unwilling, undeserving targets of a pervasive lack of social and spiritual integrity. That is why we must do all we can to move gender-variant persons out of the category of "victim" into that of "survivor" and even "thriver." But that task is certainly not easy.

Great courage and resolve are needed to reclaim our power once we have had it stolen from us. While redeveloping self-esteem and confidence in our intrinsic worth, we must look deep within ourselves to find new ways of gathering our courage. We must make this effort so we can more fully recognize and openly identify ourselves as God's beloved transgender people. As much as possible, we need to know who we are so we can effectively use our many gifts and make our contributions to the world.

It often seems that "invisibility and silence are the hallmarks of discrimination based on...gender expression."[15] We have been silent and invisible victims for too long; it's time for that discriminatory victimization to end. The open presence of gender-variant people presents a powerful theological challenge to the church. The very fact of our existence raises unavoidable ontological questions about the meaning of human life — questions that tend naturally toward topics such as justice, inclusion, and respect for our intrinsic humanity.

Thinking Christians must resolve to do whatever we can to create justice for the transgender and other oppressed minorities within the body of Christ. That's all we gender-variant people can fairly ask from the church and society: simple, evenhanded justice and equity. No special privileges — just the inalienable human right to live our lives in peace and dignity.

REHEARSING OUR WITNESS

When we have reclaimed our power and found our voice as transgender Christians and allies, we will want to bear witness in the church to four important facts:

• First, we are *not* an irrelevant, "outside" problem: we are already here inside the church. We are currently filling the pews, the choir lofts, the Sunday school classes, and even the pulpits. Many of us serve nobly and well on various church boards and committees. We are your teachers, musicians, deacons, elders, ushers, choir members, superintendents, pastors, and family members. We sit next to you or stand before you in practically every congregation on Sunday mornings. You're probably not aware that we're transgender because most of us have been forced by socioreligious oppression and fear of reprisal to hide our gender-variant orientation; but just because you don't know about us doesn't mean we don't exist and aren't a part of your life. Some of us are cross-dressers who look perfectly "normal" except when we are engaging in cross-dressing activities; others transgress gender rules by being gay, lesbian, or bisexual. Some are transsexual, intersexual, masculine women, feminine men, or transgender in some other way by some other name. Some of us are more obvious than others: a petite, delicate-featured male-to-female transsexual may look completely gender-ordinary, whereas a taller, large-boned male-to-female may look distinct or anomalous. Those of us who can "pass" and have kept silent have received the kind of welcome that brings no joy. We are all too concerned that if our transgender truths were known, our welcome might be swiftly withdrawn.

• Second, the problem of gender difference in a religious context has nothing to do with the actual presence of transgender people in the church. We have always been in the church, we are here now, and we will be in the church for as long as the church exists, although we are still mostly silent and invisible. The real religious/transgender problem is *fear*, as manifested in various forms of ignorance, bigotry, and prejudice toward us, and in our own resulting fear of rejection and/or retribution. People are afraid of what they don't understand, of that which lies outside their frame of reference. When we are confronted with fears, particularly fears of someone who is "different," we might do well to remember that faith in a loving, accepting God helps us overcome those fears. Fear can paralyze us and keep us from becoming the people we are capable of being. For example, "Martin Luther King had great reason to be afraid. He received death threats nearly every week after the Montgomery bus boycott. But King testified that he drew great solace from this simple aphorism: 'Fear knocked at the door. Faith answered. There was no one there.' "[16] The fact remains that gender-variant persons, like all other people, are blessings to the church, remarkable gifts from a loving God who appreciates human difference and who created us in wondrous diversity. Donald W. Shriver, president emeritus of Union Theological Seminary (New York), writes about the importance of "listening to the buried truth of our neighbor's suffering" as a "fundamental act of ministry."[17] Only by engaging in such basic mutual ministry with transgender people can the church cease its squandering of God's gender-variant gifts and blessings.

• Third, while it is true that gender-variant persons have been oppressed by the power structures within the church for centuries, as transgenderists we must stop perceiving ourselves as and behaving like victims. Remaining in a state of perpetual victimhood isn't going to solve our problems. We must learn how to move beyond such helpless, feeble (and often inaccurate) characterizations into the liberation and victory of our full potential as gender-gifted human beings created in the *imago Dei*. That's how we bring our gifts and make our greatest contributions to the church and to the world.

• Now here's the part that is gravely threatening to some: the Christian church must simply get used to dealing with us. We're here, we're not going away, and as more of us begin to come out publicly we will also increasingly insist upon taking our rightful role as open, active lay and ordained persons, and as equal participants in the central life of the church. God's justice requires nothing less, so the church had better get ready: change is coming, and Christians would be wise to acknowledge, affirm, and embrace those changes instead of fearing and rejecting them.

Recognizing internal pitfalls

Philosophical caring is one thing — and a very good thing; taking appropriate action to change a detrimental situation is quite another. We can criticize the system all we want, but nothing will change substantively until we develop and implement an effective plan of positive action against the entrenched, systemic, socioreligious injustices that currently exist.

In other words, we must somehow learn to stop expending all our energies on victimhood, self-pity, and criticism of the prevalent and currently existing religious system, although it's certainly necessary and even crucial to point out and define exactly what needs changing before we can take appropriate, liberating action. Also, we must cease clinging to any naïve belief that the system, as embodied by the present institutional and universal church, is somehow blameless and incorruptible. (The church's heavily publicized struggles with sexual abuse by clergy ought to be sufficient proof of that!) Much work is to be done, and many situations within the corridors of our social and religious institutions are crying for change.

Not that all transgenderists have simply wrung their hands in self-pitying victimhood. On the contrary, transgender activists like Leslie Feinberg, author Jamison Greene, and Riki Ann Wilchins have organized groups, addressed the larger society in their books and essays, and traveled all over the country seeking to educate people about the need for significant change in our society's gender assumptions. Yet even the brilliant transsexual Kate Bornstein, who has performed her transgender "edutainment" (i.e., educational entertainment) in many universities and nightclubs, told Virginia in early 2001 that up until then, most transgenderist work had been focused on deconstruction of the current system and attitudes. What was then needed, according to Bornstein, was to begin the reconstruction of a more just society — including a spiritual or religious vision to provide the necessary inspiration and cohesion.

Accordingly, after we've identified and documented the problem areas, the "appropriate directions of change" (and, as we've said, there are many), we must determine exactly how to go about creating positive, beneficial spiritual transformation within our religious belief systems and our faith communities. Because we are the experts on our own oppression, we are the ones who must take the lead in devising effective solutions to our problems. That's a monumental assignment, one that will take time, effort, and an unshakeable desire to see justice done — but it's essential if we are to make progress for transgender persons (and, therefore, for *all* persons, regardless of gender) within the church and the rest of society. It's an intimidating, daunting, and often demoralizing task to take on the entrenched power of an institution like the church, but we must find ways to unite our efforts and energies in working to do just that if we want to create the necessary changes.

We all have weaknesses and flaws, we all make mistakes, and we all sometimes fall short in our efforts to see justice done. We who are white inevitably profit from the systemic racism of our world, we who live in the United States inevitably profit from the economic exploitation of other countries and the natural environment, and so forth. We err if we imagine ourselves to be innocent, with all that is evil located somewhere outside ourselves. However, we must not let our own failings dissuade us from doing what we can whenever we can. We cannot allow any temporary obstacle, human frailty, or fear of reprisal to keep us from moving inexorably toward the creation of God's holy justice upon the earth.

Thomas Edison made several thousand attempts to invent the electric lightbulb before he finally achieved success. Imagine where we'd all be if he'd become discouraged or disgusted and stopped his work (probably in the dark!). Film director John McTiernan has said, "Lack of failure is clear evidence of being an absolute genius or being a coward."[18] We don't pretend to be even part-time geniuses, but we don't want to be cowards either. That leaves us no legitimate alternative but to keep trying, to keep coming out to others, to keep on discussing and writing and speaking and working and loving others and living openly with integrity. If we are faithful, eventually a just church and a just world for all of God's oppressed and marginalized human beings, including transgender people, will become a living reality.

Learning to walk with God through change

Right now God seems to be acting within the church and within the lives of people, stirring up in our hearts a longing for justice. Many of the old, unworkable paradigms, assumptions, and other myths that once dominated our theology and our thinking about "mainline" religion and culture are failing.

For many on the religious or political right, the rate of change is terrifying. Some thinkers cite President Eisenhower's 1954 domino theory — that the collapse of one state leads to the consecutive collapse of neighboring states — to argue that it is dangerous to tamper with any traditional custom or attitude, however unjust it may be. "Do not remove the ancient landmark/that your ancestors set up,"[19] these people insist, using an out-of-context biblical phrase about respecting real-estate property markers to justify their fear of changes that might advance the cause of equal justice for everyone. When property markers become more important than creating justice for human beings, something is dreadfully wrong.

Yet at the same time many people are hungry for genuine spiritual connectedness and right relationship. They are seeking new ways to live in an awareness of contemporary theological understanding, using increasingly enlightened hermeneutics (i.e., interpretive tools and frameworks) that continually develop and progress as new knowledge becomes available to us. Biblical scholars probe the frontiers of scriptural inquiry and exegesis, while other theologians and laypeople carefully consider the meaning of Christian identity and witness in a world that is fractured and diverse.[20] Yes, a more interdependent world culture is emerging (at least in terms of technology, communication, and economics), but that global culture can and does generate dangerous new forms of exploitation and injustice. We who claim the name "Christian" must prepare ourselves to meet these formidable new challenges. We must attempt to understand the diverse, complex nature of our increasingly globalized existence, and we must somehow learn to live side by side in peace with all of our sisters and brothers even as we try to make sense of the world and our place in it. Creating gender justice within the institution of Christianity can provide us with excellent practice and perhaps a few inches of progress in the struggle toward global justice for everyone.

According to Micah 6:8, God tells us how to cooperate with the will of our creator, even in transitional times like ours: We are to do justice, and to love mercy, and to walk humbly with our God. It is worth noting that Micah speaks of walking *with* God, not *after* or *under* God, and not in abject, mindless obedience *to* God. Because God's essence is love, s/he is the love and yearning for justice that is within us, flowing between us as we work together toward a more relational, less alienated world. Nevertheless, especially in these unsettling days of confusion and even raw anger at the "differences" we may perceive in others, we often discover that loving the ideas of justice and mercy is much easier than acting decisively upon them. We, Vanessa and Virginia, consider walking with God (and hence in solidarity with all who receive us) to be the top priority for any life of spiritual authenticity. If we can all learn to do that, then surely committing acts of justice and mercy will become the natural and logically manifested extensions of our lives. As United Methodist bishop Kenneth Carder has remarked, the God with whom we are called to walk humbly is a God who sees the misery of the oppressed, hears the cries of the abused and violated, and knows the suffering of the poor. "Only a persistent walk with this God will lead us toward justice, mercy, and humility."[21]

The challenges and dangers before us are great, but so too are the opportunities and rewards for those who have the courage to become personally involved in the struggle to embrace our full humanity in all its remarkable diversity. Because of our inability to achieve a socially approved "normalcy" (whatever *that* is), we who are gender-variant are particularly well suited to the tasks of spiritual skepticism — of adopting a hermeneutic of suspicion about "the way things have always been done" within the context of our faith. Please understand that we're not talking about being skeptical of God's message of love and acceptance as contained in Scripture and modeled for us in the life of Jesus; we're referring instead to the misuse of religion and the enforced binary gender construct as abusive tools of oppression. We want to encourage a healthy, spiritually focused skepticism that supports and promotes an in-depth questioning of religious and social authorities (or, at the very least, a refusal to engage in blind obedience for the sake of convenience). Spiritual skepticism also engenders reflection on the many difficult and critical issues of injustice that bear highly significant implications for the church, for society, and for our world.

To create justice is to do the prophetic work of God on earth, and we Christians are directly called to engage ourselves in this holy endeavor. The choice to answer that call is ours. Our responses to God's summons will influence and ultimately determine the future of the institutional Christian church in the twenty-first century, including its relevance and global effectiveness.

Having reordered some of our intellectual and attitudinal equipment for a gender-justice journey, now would seem to be a good time to share the personal stories of Virginia's and Vanessa's travels thus far. Read on. . . .

Chapter 3

VIRGINIA RAMEY MOLLENKOTT'S GENDER-VARIANT JOURNEY

I WAS SIXTY-FOUR YEARS OLD before I became fully conscious of the fact that I am a masculine woman, and that the deepest oppression I have known stemmed not simply from being female, nor even from being lesbian, but from being a gender transgressor. How could I not have known?

I remember reading Margaret Atwood's great novel *The Handmaid's Tale* when it was first published in 1985. Having grown up in a Protestant fundamentalist context, I found Atwood's plotline horrifying but plausible. Yes, fundamentalists *could* take over the United States by killing all elected officials and placing the blame on foreign terrorists. And yes, they would then be free to seize power and suspend the human and civil rights of all women and any men who opposed them. Once women's bank accounts had been placed under the control of men, and women had been forbidden to work gainfully outside the home, the total enslavement of women could be easy enough, and meaningful sexual relationships would be impossible. Of course there would be secret clubs where powerful men could engage in sleazy sex, but for most people love of any sort would become a thing of the past.

GENDER TRANSGRESSION

I was particularly horrified to read in *The Handmaid's Tale* that anyone engaging in same-sex love would be executed, then hanged by the neck on the fence of Harvard Yard, with a sign proclaiming that this was the just punishment of a "gender transgressor." Recently the chief justice of Alabama's Supreme Court, a Southern Baptist in good standing, said that the state carries the right to confine or even to execute, and must use that power in order to prevent the subversion of children into homosexuality. His statement received strong praise from the religious right.[1] So as much as I would like to say that in this regard Margaret Atwood's novel is implausible, I cannot do so.

Back in 1985 I was puzzled that the signs on those executed for same-sex activity in Atwood's novel read not "homosexual," but "gender transgressor." But now I understand that well before the current transgender liberation movement, Margaret Atwood saw that the real offense of homosexuality is that it undercuts society's binary gender construct: the supposition that "normal" genitals carry with them "normal" masculine or feminine interests and behaviors, including sexual attraction exclusively to the "opposite" sex. Gender goes even deeper than sexual orientation in the collective psyche, and the deepest reason for blocking gay, lesbian, and bisexual liberation is to preserve traditional power arrangements, especially male primacy and female subordination.[2] Consequently, I have argued in *Omnigender* and elsewhere that far from being a mere tagalong to gay, lesbian, and bisexual liberation, transgender liberation is absolutely central to the entire movement.

Masculine gay men or feminine lesbian women — and there are many — have very little to fear from homophobes unless they are very public about their homosexuality. The effeminate gay males and the masculine lesbians are the especially endangered ones, because by our very existence we raise questions about the social construction of gender and the power accorded to males and masculinity.

EARLY CHILDHOOD TRANS-SYMPTOMS

Again: Why did it take me so long to come to these realizations? Certainly I knew in early childhood I was "different." I loved my brother's toy cars, trucks, and cowboy guns and had no time for playing with dolls. Whenever dolls were given to me, I put them to bed for permanent naps and never touched them again. I constantly drew pictures of boys or men and wanted to be a missionary surgeon when

I grew up. (I had heard from missionaries that overseas, women could take leadership positions because very few men wanted to live under the conditions they had to endure.) I hated wearing skirts, but jeans and slacks were considered "boys' clothing" in my fundamentalist household, so in spite of my protests I was required to wear dresses or skirts. My mother, grandmother, and aunts were constantly on my case about keeping my knees together and standing up straight. I took great offense at the gender put-downs the neighbor boys used on us girls, such as their chanting of "The girls in France wear tissue paper pants." Why did I care so much *what* the girls in France wore or didn't wear? Ah — but I knew this was a way of mocking us females as vulnerable prey, and I hated it.

Instinctively I adopted a "masculine" mode of courage. My older brother, being something of a sissy, was often targeted by the local bullies, but I defended him with my fists and derived satisfaction from hearing the bullies grunt with surprise when I landed a few solid punches. When some older boys put a live snake around my neck, I stood my ground stoically, pretending that I was not the least bit disturbed, although inwardly I was shuddering as the snake crawled across my shoulders and arms. The boys, getting no satisfaction, eventually removed the snake and never bothered me again. I was gratified to hear their assessment of me as they walked away: "She's tough!"

From ages four to nine I had a special girlfriend named Mary Lou for whom I would have walked through fire and with whom I spent every available moment. When Mary Lou and I played house, I was the daddy and she the mother, while the other girls got stuck with being the children. When a particular bully interrupted our game once too often, I pushed him into a sticky bush and we all ran for home to the tune of his howls of rage and humiliation.

At church I was given to understand that only men were permitted to preach and teach the Bible, but in my home neighborhood I preached the gospel to any kids who would listen. In private I also practiced making speeches, timing myself to see how long I could hold forth without saying anything I considered silly, stupid, or awkward. When I turned out to be lacking in talent during my piano lessons, my mother finally took mercy and sent me to elocution lessons instead.

Elocution is a word I rarely hear anymore, and when I do, it usually carries a negative shading, implying that the public speaker has a studiously artificial style. But at ages eight and nine, I felt those elocution lessons to be a welcome relief from piano practice and especially the recitals, with their mandatory and humiliating curtsies.

A DIFFERENT CONTEXT

When I was nine, my father left home. My mother, brother, and I moved from our all-white neighborhood into the tenderloin district of Philadelphia, where at school we white children were a tiny minority. This was the mid-1940s, when big cities were experiencing a great deal of racial unrest, and one day as I left school by myself after cleaning the blackboards, I was beaten with lead pipes by a large gang of African American kids. Fortunately I was able to fight my way back into the school before I was killed. I was never treated for my physical injuries, and to this day I suffer from that beating. As a girl, I would have been permitted to express great fear and pain after this incident, but unconsciously I had picked up on male socialization. I kept a stiff upper lip.

At about age ten I chose my "life verse" from the Bible, as we Plymouth Brethren children were encouraged to do. The passage I chose showed my identification with the apostle Paul, who was adored in the Plymouth Brethren assemblies but not considered a proper role model for a mere girl. The life verse I picked still seems relevant to me, despite the crippling arthritis that makes the competitive athletic imagery seem rather ironic: "This one thing I do: forgetting what lies behind and straining forward to what lies ahead, I press on toward the goal for the prize of the heavenly call of God in Christ Jesus" (Phil. 3:13–14).

It must have been about the same time that I copied into the flyleaf of my Bible the following poem:

> Men may misjudge thy aim,
> Think they have cause to blame,
> Say, Thou art wrong.

Keep on the quiet way,
Christ is the judge, not they.
Fear not, be strong.

Fearless strength and independence were hardly the attributes that were being urged upon us girls; in fact, I was explicitly taught never to win in any competition with boys, and never to do anything for myself if a man was available to do it for me. Clearly on some level I was rejecting those messages. I was also preparing myself for the negative judgments I would encounter when I grew older and became a controversial figure.

At age eleven I entered into a love relationship with a twenty-one-year-old woman from our church. Technically, of course, she was committing statutory rape, but from my perspective everything was consensual. It felt wonderful to be loved and to love. But I hated it when I began to develop breasts, and slumped so badly trying to hide them that the family forced me to wear an extremely uncomfortable shoulder brace.

HIGH SCHOOL AND COLLEGE

When Mother discovered my relationship, she packed me off to the Southern Presbyterian high school mentioned in chapter 1. The students there were remarkably kind to me, many secretly becoming good friends despite being warned that I was a dangerous lesbian, inclined toward rape. The faculty and administration persecuted me on a regular basis. I was embarrassed by being assigned to someone who would teach me how to iron my dresses like a proper girl, and infuriated to find out that one faculty member had been ransacking my closet and bureau to uncover any nefarious somethings that might be concealed therein. I was accused of forcibly stripping a girl, a ludicrous accusation in a school where dormitory nakedness shocked me. (Was unabashed nakedness a southern thing? I was astonished by it.) I was punished for that made-up infraction by several years of hard labor in the school laundry and kitchen. After my suicide attempt, I was confined to the school infirmary and required to read a book about the devil. I still remember the title: *Whom Resist.*

When I went to college at Bob Jones University, I was astonished at the rigid discipline and deeply dismayed at the gender rules that forced young women to wear nylon stockings even when we were playing tennis. (The only reason we were ever given for that rule was that our legs didn't look good without them!) I sensed the same duplicity on campus that I had noticed in high school: If you were popular with someone powerful, you could get away with plenty; woe unto you if you were straightforwardly your own person. I remember one very masculine lesbian at the college — her nickname was Butch! — who dared to whistle her admiration of various women on campus because she was favored by the dean of women and had a protected status that I never achieved. Still, I worked hard, lived celibate, earned top grades, and was invited to return to teach literature and write a daily radio program.

One year of that was enough. When I heard the college president telling the assembled faculty that we had no right so much as to think a thought that differed from his, I knew that I had to leave. That realization brought with it a serious dilemma. In my church and family, the only way a woman could choose to live anywhere except with her mother was to be married. I knew I was lesbian, but I had been assured by the one professor in whom I had confided that if I married heterosexually and pretended to be a heterosexual, eventually I would become heterosexual. I didn't really believe that, but I desperately hoped that by some miracle it might be true.

MARRIAGE, MOTHERHOOD, AND DIVORCE

So at age twenty-one I married Fred Mollenkott and began my seventeen and a half years of living a lie. Fred died young, of leukemia, like so many of the Pacific World War II veterans who were downwind from the atomic bombs, and I do not want to speak ill of him. But the combination of my lesbian and transgender orientations, Fred's inability to open himself to intimacy, and the androcentric theology both of us had been taught guaranteed that the marriage was hopeless from the start. Fred often told me that if I were a *normal* woman, I would delight in serving his every whim; to him, joyful obedience to men was a sign of normal Christian femininity. And in the 1950s and early 1960s (a very retrograde period for American women), he had the whole force of social attitudes on his side. Because of that, and because of my growing awareness of my gender variance, his judgments fell upon me like a mantle of lead.

At twenty-six, hoping against hope that it would somehow improve our marriage, I gave birth to a son. From the fifth month of my pregnancy onward, the obstetrician assured me that I was carrying a girl, and I was terrified that I would have no idea of how to socialize her. (That feeling alone should have told me I was transgender, but no such concept was available to me at the time; where there are no words, there can be no conscious realizations.) When Paul emerged I was tremendously relieved, confident that I could socialize a son to be a fully human being. With the help of God and many others, I did. Paul is now a gentle and loving father to three beautiful little girls. When his one-year-old was crying recently, I heard him crooning to her very softly the Barney song, "I love you / you love me / we're a happy family." Because Corrine adores Barney, she quieted right down.

Miserable though marriage to Fred was, I thought that divorce was forever forbidden to me by Scripture. (Ironically, many Christians uphold what they claim are biblical prohibitions against homosexuality and transgenderism but permit divorce and remarriage. Yet Jesus explicitly condemned divorce as it was constituted in his day, and never condemned homosexuality or transgenderism. So much for the church's obedience to Jesus' insights!)[3]

Although my parents were divorced, my mother never had her day in court, never consented to the divorce, and never remarried; she saw herself as the injured party and my father as the guilty one. Consequently, I thought I was required to stay with Fred forevermore: in Mother's words, having made my bed, I had to lie in it. All through that time I had been teaching college literature and working on a Ph.D., and my dissertation advisor urged me to research and write on Milton and the Apocrypha. Not only did my work win New York University's award for that year's best doctoral dissertation in the field of English, it introduced me to Milton's biblical arguments in favor of divorce for incompatibility.[4] From Milton I learned how to read the Bible in a liberating way, and when Fred began to take out his frustrations on Paul, I broke for freedom. First I moved to a state college that would not fire me for the divorce; then Paul and I moved out, and I filed to end the marriage.

ADULT TRANSGENDERISM

By the early 1970s I was living as a closeted lesbian mother and becoming more feminist by the minute as I studied the Bible with the hermeneutical tools I had learned from Milton and various graduate courses. In 1975 I delivered a biblical case for male-female equality at the first national conference of the Evangelical Women's Caucus.[5] That speech was subsequently published in *Sojourners* and then expanded into my book *Women, Men, and the Bible*. Next came the book I coauthored with Letha Dawson Scanzoni, *Is the Homosexual My Neighbor? A Positive Christian Response*.

As I began to speak at dozens of church and academic conferences around the country, many right-wingers tried to discredit my message by raising questions about my sexual orientation. Looking back, I find it fascinating that so many of the attacks were more gender-related than orientational: "Why is your hair so short?" or "Why do you feminists always look so plain?" or "Why don't you at least *try* to look pretty?"

Increasingly unable to tolerate skirts, I tried wearing floor-length caftans; but those too were objects of suspicion. What a relief it was, once I was "out" as a lesbian, to give away all my dresses and skirts and use pantsuits for teaching and speaking engagements!

Once, when traveling in England, I was blocked by a male security guard from entering the women's room until I was able to convince him of my actual gender. Later, thinking about that experience, I realized that in all my life no male had ever spoken to me with quite the measure of respect that the security guard had accorded to me when he thought I was male like him. Apparently men receive more respect from one another even during a reprimand than women receive from men at any time whatsoever!

Sometime in the mid-1980s my partner and I were walking arm-in-arm in New York City when a man spat full in my face. At the time we assumed he was expressing his opinion of homosexuality (13 percent of gay men and lesbians have been spat upon). But now that I am savvier about gender, I realize it was my female masculinity that disgusted him. After all, many heterosexual women walk arm-in-arm; he had no way of knowing we were lesbians.

One other incident comes to mind from a transgender perspective. When I was going through a very difficult period of my life in the mid-1990s, recently single after sixteen years with a woman I deeply loved, my psychotherapist floated the idea that perhaps, like various other spiritual leaders, I might prefer to live celibate. I quickly assured her that no, on the contrary, I had found that living in partnership stabilized and energized my ministry. I went on to say that I felt open to a partner of any sex and gender: a tender and nurturing male would be as acceptable to me as another woman. To my surprise, the therapist (a heterosexual Jamaican black woman) became exceedingly upset: "Why would you say a thing like that?" As I was leaving she uncharacteristically returned to the topic: "Don't do anything about partnering with a man without consulting me first!"

Pondering the intensity of her reaction, I realize that it too was gender-based. Why would a masculine lesbian in her mid-sixties even *consider* taking up with a man? To my therapist, the fact that I might capitalize on my admittedly small bisexual component was unthinkable, as was the fact that many people would no doubt have assumed we were a gay male couple. (Long ago, when a gay man took me to a predominantly male bar, a man propositioned me but withdrew in shock when I told him I wasn't the gender he was seeking.)

I am happy to report that not many months after my brief bisexual foray, God brought into my life a tender and wise woman named Suzannah Tilton. She had read the first edition of *Is the Homosexual My Neighbor?* years before, and came to hear me when I was speaking near her home in North Carolina. After we had become friends but before we made a life commitment, Suzannah told me that my mode of self-presentation was "quite masculine," and lent me her copy of Leslie Feinberg's novel *Stone Butch Blues*. In that novel I saw my own transgender identity writ large. Although I never took male hormones in order to pass as male, I felt the way Jess did at the end of the novel: To be simply male was *not* what she wanted, and to be simply female was for her quite impossible. She was *neither* male nor female, in one sense, and *both* in another. While she had been passing as male behind a hormone-induced beard, s/he had realized that his/her face "no longer revealed the contrasts of [his/her] full gender"; she had been unable to "recognize the he-she" that was the only gender identification that felt authentic. Fortunately, unlike Jess and his/her transgender friend Ruth, Suzannah and I were not afraid to go out together, nor are we afraid to live in partnership together. But that is partly the result of the work of Leslie Feinberg and others in the transgender revolution that is currently under way.

People are still afraid of ambiguity. Indeed, since the terrorist attacks of September 11, 2001, airport security checkpoints have become dangerous for transgenderists, one masculine woman even being forced to lower her pants to her thighs in public, right next to the x-ray machine, on the pretense that she was a possible security risk. (The point here is not that women could not pose a security risk, but that guards do not tend to focus on gender-conformists, but on gender-variant people.) In such cases, the transgender person has no "proper authorities" to turn to for help, because the perpetrators *are* the "proper authorities," genderphobes who are backed up by a national guardsman with an M-16.[6] Suzannah and I are grateful that so far no such indignities have been visited upon us, perhaps because of our advanced age. Also, whenever I can see in somebody's eyes that they are dealing with my gender ambiguity, I am careful to smile in order to reassure them that whatever it is, it's friendly.

THE CULTURAL MAPPING OF SEX/GENDER

All this brings me back to that question I have asked several times already: Why did it take so many years to realize that transgender phobia runs even deeper than homophobia, so that my masculine womanhood was even more deeply offensive than my lesbianism?

My father, who as I write is ninety-nine and going strong, has always defended against my many similarities to himself by calling me embarrassing endearments that emphasize traditional femininity, such as "Doll." Yet it took Feinberg's description of "butch" humiliation at being forced to wear dresses as the price of admission to a funeral of one of their friends to make me realize that I too am "butch." Why was I so slow? Because all of society has conspired to keep such awareness latent and buried in unconsciousness.

On our cultural map of sex/gender,[7] only the far west of male heterosexual masculinity and the far east of female heterosexual femininity have been fully but inaccurately detailed. The entire central area of transgenderism (including intersexuality, transsexuality, homosexuality, cross-dressing, and the like) has been left blank, with the exception of a few celebrity names and a few negative stereotypes that now remind me of annotations in the blank spots of ancient maps: "There be monsters here." Only as society has begun to allow mixed-gender bodies to become more visible on our sex/gender map have the parameters of what the culture can recognize begun to shift. Once people become sufficiently aware of biological, psychological, and orientational deviations from the statistical norms, we will become able to recognize "in-between" people as natural. The fact is that for years I could neither conceptualize nor accept my transgender identity because I lacked the words to make myself culturally intelligible — even to myself! For that reason there is present such an urgent present need for transgenderists to stand up, be counted, and speak the truth of their own experience — especially in the Christian community, where (alas!) so much transphobia has been able to find religious validation.

THE GENESIS CREATION STORIES

A second and closely related reason that it took me so long to "come home" to my transgender reality is the theology I was taught. Like the entire right wing of Judaism, Christianity, and Islam today, the Plymouth Brethren relied on the scriptural creation stories for their sex/gender attitudes. Because God created Adam and Eve, not

Adam and Steve, same-sex activity was forever prohibited; every sane person knew that there are just exactly two genders, male and female. Moreover, because Eve was called the "helpmeet" of Adam, every reasonable person must recognize that women were created to serve men. Never mind that the Hebrew phrase *ezer neged* (usually translated "helpmeet" or "helper") means "a power equal to."

Never mind also that Adam (the Earth creature) was originally created androgynous or intersexual, both male and female, until God placed that creature into a deep sleep and divided him/her into the human male and female as we know them (Gen. 2:21–24). Never mind that both male and female were made in the image of the One Divine Source, who must therefore encompass both male and female within his/her nature (Gen. 1:27). Never mind that Jesus, called the express image of God, is depicted as born of a virgin, so that like all parthenogenetic births in other species, Jesus would have been chromosomally female all his/her life.[8] Never mind that the biblical authors utilize female and nature imagery concerning God, amid the predominantly male imagery that reflected their own patriarchal backgrounds.[9]

Never mind all of that: according to the religious right's interpretation of Genesis 1 and 2, all intersexual babies must receive medical intervention to make them conform to clear-cut male or female patterning; transsexuals must remain in their sex/gender of birth in submission to God's will, however agonizing; homosexuals must live in enforced celibacy, however lonely; bisexuals must truncate all same-sex attractions, however diminishing; women must accept only supportive and secondary roles, however self-denying; cross-dressers must cease and desist from cross-dressing, however painful; and everyone must forego any interests, behaviors, or sex/gender presentations that challenge whatever their given society happens to assign as properly masculine or feminine. (Those transpeople wealthy enough to move to a society better suited to their propensities could presumably evade many judgments by doing so — although right-wing Christian missionaries have tended to conflate the gospel with their own social customs, so that even moving might not really help.)

THE CHRISTIAN SCRIPTURES HONOR
A TRANSGENDER PROPHET

When I was young, it would have given me enormous courage had I known that not just once but twice the New Testament honors a transgender and homoerotic prophet by quoting him in a positive context. But in fact I have made the discovery only during the preparation of this book. I am referring to Epimenides, a poet and prophet who lived in Knossos, Crete, in the sixth century B.C.E.[10] The Jerusalem Bible, the Wycliffe Bible Commentary, and other reliable works identify Epimenides as the source of two statements by the apostle Paul, one located in Acts 17:28 and the other in Titus 1:12.

According to Greek sources, Epimenides was the shaman who successfully helped to rid Athens of a plague and who assisted the Athenian statesman Solon in his famous reforms, including the institutionalization of homoerotic love as it was practiced in Crete.[11] In his book *Greek Divination* (1913), William R. Holliday compares Epimenides to the transgender shaman Tiresias, who changed sex several times and whose clothing was simultaneously "masculine" and "feminine."

Knowing all this, and knowing his learned audience would know all this, the apostle Paul twice quotes Epimenides to buttress his own argument. In fact, in the epistle to Titus, Paul goes so far as to call Epimenides a prophet! I was told all my life that the Hebrew and Christian Scriptures are unanimously negative about gay, lesbian, and bisexual experience, and I was profoundly shamed because of my transgender characteristics. How *stunned,* and then how *liberated* I would have felt to be told that one of my kind had been featured favorably in the canon of sacred Scripture!

If I had known about Epimenides when I was a teenager, and if I had found the nerve to share my discovery with the elders of the church, I know what they would have said. They would have denied that Paul could possibly have known about Epimenides' homosexuality and transgenderism. If I had pressed the issue, pointing out that an omniscient God certainly knew even if Paul didn't, then I would have been "read out of the meeting," the Plymouth

Brethren equivalent of excommunication. Still, the knowledge would have been wonderful because I was smart enough to figure out that to the degree that a person considers the Bible to be divinely inspired and authoritative, to the same degree the person is obligated to acknowledge that a gay transgender shaman is profoundly honored in the canon of Scripture. That knowledge alone would have been enough of a ray of hope to prevent my suicide attempt, because the Bible was absolutely central to my worldview.

It would also have provided hope for me to have known that Epimenides is not the only gay, lesbian, bisexual, or transgender person who is treated with respect and honor in the Bible.[12] For instance, in her computerized Bible Pat Conover found forty-nine uses of the explicit term "eunuch," not counting other descriptive phrases signifying eunuchs. Modern English translations use the term only about a dozen times, preferring nongendered terms like "official" that obscure the "third-sex" or gender-variant nature of the people being discussed.[13] Nevertheless, it remains clear that whereas eunuchs of faith are rejected in Deuteronomy 23:1, they are fully welcomed by Isaiah (56:3–5) and by Philip (Acts 8), and are singled out for praise by Jesus in Matthew 19. So I now proceed on my transgender journey deeply reassured by the biblical honoring of Epimenides and other gender-variant people. Despite my early training, I know now that I am deeply loved by the one who made me as different as I am and who in turn loves the world through my particularities.

OMNIGENDERING

At any rate, I knew none of those liberating realizations early on, and I was sixty-four years old before I grasped the fact that I am a masculine woman and therefore a gender transgressor. I wrote *Omnigender* to help myself and others begin to construct a religious and spiritual vision to undergird the transgender movement. It is certainly my most radical book, inasmuch as it gets at the *radix,* the root of our culture's gender crisis. Ironically, judging from remarks on the Internet, the thing that has most horrified readers on the right has been my remark that I despised wearing dresses. (The irony there is that many heterosexual and traditionally feminine women also prefer to wear pants most of the time.) Either those Internet commentators haven't really read the book, or they missed the point, or they focused on that minor matter as an outlet for their transgender phobia.

After my former editor at The Pilgrim Press told me he wanted me to have a portrait taken for the jacket of *Omnigender,* I wore my usual garb but was careful not to smile because I had noticed that men in "power portraits" rarely smile, whereas women usually do. Apparently my strategy worked; a Canadian poet with whom I exchange books wrote that the photograph "makes a strong political statement." Several friends have told me that when people first see the portrait, they ask whether the subject is male or female. I hope that in every case the answer was "Technically, a woman; but spiritually, both."

Chapter 4

VANESSA SHERIDAN'S GENDER-VARIANT JOURNEY

A GROWING NUMBER of Christians seem to intuitively understand and agree that exclusivity and other forms of injustice within the church are wrong. They understand that the church of Jesus Christ should be an open, welcoming place for all people. Some of them are even acutely aware that sexual and gender minorities have long been the targets of unwarranted oppression within the institution of Christianity. These people know that addressing such issues is paramount for thinking Christians if we are to take seriously the work of creating justice for all people. A few courageous souls are even beginning to speak out boldly about the church's continuing injustice in gender/sexual matters, and they are becoming active in the attempt to change the institution's attitudes and behaviors in this regard. I hope, in all humility, to be one such proactive person.

In this chapter I share some of my own story because I'm convinced there is a remarkable power in the validity of narrative and in the authenticity of one's personal experience. The account of Virginia's gender journey in the preceding chapter is proof enough of that for me. Subjectively speaking, my journey to this point has not been as remarkable as Virginia's. I doubt that my life will ever make as powerful an impact on the world as hers, but it is the only life I have; it's the one I was given and the one I have lived. Also, while I deeply respect Virginia's decision to share much personal information about her sexuality and its extensive ramifications for her life, I have decided to confine my own narrative solely to the elements of transgenderism that have affected me so profoundly.

MY BEGINNINGS

I am a male-to-female cross-dresser and am proud to be so, although that was not always the case. I was raised in the southeastern United States, in the conservative buckle of the Bible Belt. I distinctly remember feeling that I was "different" when I was two or three. I certainly didn't understand what that difference meant on any sort of cognitive level, and I didn't have words to describe my internal difference, but I was aware, at least on some level, that my transgender self existed even in those very early years. However, I quickly intuited that it wouldn't be prudent to discuss my feelings and concerns about this type of difference with anyone in my family or church.

I am the product of a highly conservative, deeply fundamentalist, extremely traditional, and very patriarchal upbringing within the religious context of the Southern Baptist Convention. Like many who have grown up in that particular culture, my family was in church practically every time the doors were open. Little southern boys (and, one presumes, many little northern, eastern, and western boys as well) who had an innate desire to express a more feminine persona weren't exactly encouraged toward adopting transgender behavior or identification by the institutional church or the rest of society. I was taught that gender/sex roles and expectations were clearly delineated by God in the Bible, and that the job of the church and society was to enforce God's will in these matters. This "divinely ordained" structure was never to be questioned or altered in any way, shape, or form. I hid my true gender-variant self from the world, learning to be ashamed and to reject and repress an important part of who I was.

I discovered that I was never supposed to express any doubt or skepticism about the patriarchal teachings of our religious belief system. Conformity of thought and behavior was the rule and the expectation. I was to obey the church's teachings and accept their ensuing socioreligious implications for my life without question. I tried my best to live up to the tenets of our Southern Baptist church, no matter how difficult or unrealistic that effort ultimately proved to be. I truly wanted to be a good boy, one who loved Jesus and the biblical literalist faith community to which my family belonged. To be perfectly honest, though, that effort toward conformity and obedience often originated more from a religious sense of duty and an underlying fear of punishment than anything else. All the while, because I was convinced I had to sublimate, disguise, and even disown the truth about my gender-variant human essence, my very soul was slowly being eaten away.

My internal transgender nature and orientation, not to mention my gender-variant spirituality, were strongly at odds with what I experienced in my church upbringing: an unyielding religious legalism, an insistent emphasis on homogeneity and unity of religious thought and behavior, and a constant negativity toward any sort of "difference." The awkward juxtaposition of this rigid belief system and my internal gender-based awareness created a certain degree of what psychology calls "cognitive dissonance" on various emotional, psychological, and spiritual levels. What I was feeling and experiencing in terms of gender just wasn't lining up with what my mind was being taught.

The growing conundrum became especially relevant for me around the age of thirteen when, to my surprise and alarm, I stumbled upon what I assumed to be a very specific and unassailable condemnation of cross-dressing in Scripture. My literalist interpretation of Deuteronomy 22:5 ("A woman shall not wear a man's apparel, nor shall a man put on a woman's garment, for whoever does such things is abhorrent to the Lord your God.") was not exactly conducive toward any sort of healthy transgender self-acceptance. I had no idea about an informed exegesis of Old Testament Holiness Codes nor did I know anything about contextual theology, a state of ignorance that created tremendous anxiety for me in the ensuing years. To say I remained theologically naïve is to be rather generous; frankly, I was dumber than a six-foot soil sample in terms of any genuine theological understanding or compelling spiritual insight. I simply and naïvely internalized the literal words of Deuteronomy as true and personally condemning. My gender-variant spirit suffered greatly as a direct result of that negative, highly damaging scriptural interpretation.

INTERPRETIVE DIFFERENCES

I have since learned that selective literalist interpretations of the Bible can be very dangerous. Literalism effectively prevents us from applying valid, life-affirming principles of Scripture in the light of accumulated human wisdom, modern thought and inquiry, scientific information and discoveries, and an ever-evolving sociocultural awareness. Selective biblical literalism also precludes us from achieving a more insightful, comprehensive, and universal perspective on spiritual principles.

Selective literalism tends to isolate Scripture, boxing it up within a particular social or chronological interpretive context, then awkwardly applying it in ways that are not particularly useful for contemporary spiritual growth or understanding. For example, the Holiness Codes of the Hebrew Scriptures were specific sets of instructions written to and for a specific people for ostensibly specific reasons at a specific time in history. Our twenty-first-century Christian context and our improved scientific insights are radically different from those of the Israelites wandering through the Sinai wilderness thousands of years ago. Therefore, an honest, useful, and contemporary interpretation of the many legalistic religious injunctions specific to those particular people in that place and in that time should require careful consideration in the light of our greater scientific knowledge, vastly different cultural situation, and increased theological awareness. Ignoring or minimizing such cultural advances and enlightened interpretive understandings is a disservice to God, the Bible, and ourselves.

For example, the Bible tells us that the following are wrong: eating shellfish (Deut. 14:9–10), having tattoos (Lev. 19:28), wearing blended cloth (Deut. 22:11), not having a fence around one's roof (Deut. 22:8), women having authority over men (1 Cor. 11:3; 1 Tim. 2:11–15; it's interesting to note here how women are to attain their salvation), men having long hair and women having short hair (1 Cor. 5–7), and women wearing pearls or braiding their hair (1 Tim. 2:9). The Bible condones slavery (Eccles. 2:7; Eph. 6:5) and genocide (1 Sam. 15) as well, just to mention a few other things that are supposedly sanctioned in Scripture.

In truth, the Bible is not some mystical rulebook of do's and don'ts that magically fell out of heaven to be slavishly adhered to in every time, culture, or situation. The Bible is no abstract work of fiction or conjecture, and it's certainly not just a book. It is a living thing, a message of great meaning and significance for our twenty-first-century lives, a dynamic entity that is only enhanced by the passage of time.

The Bible says many things that were specific for a time or a culture or a people; in the Bible's case, these things were directly addressed to the ancient Hebrews of several millennia ago for specific reasons. That's why we must always read and examine biblical passages from within their appropriate context and interpret them intelligently if we are to derive appropriate meanings and implications for our contemporary lives.

Many people have read these passages while applying the tenets of disciplined scholarship in an effort to better understand the Scriptures. They have looked back to the original texts, trying to be more aware of the culture that was prevalent at the time the passages were written. We now have women in pulpits; we wear poly-cotton blends in our clothing; we see many women with short hair (uncovered in church, no less); we see men with long hair; we have abolished slavery, and so on. To try and create some divine mandate against transgender expression demands that one must just as uncompromisingly adhere to all the rest of the written law while condemning the above-listed acts — that is, if you want to avoid stooping to extreme hypocrisy. For what it's worth, my simple advice (offered solely in the spirit of altruism and love) is that we stop messing with people and start dealing with our own issues. We should try doing what Jesus recommended: Remove the plank from our own eye before going after the speck in our neighbor's eye (Matt. 7:3–5; Luke 6:41–42). In other words, let's make sure our personal vision is clear before we attack someone else's.

Personal struggles

With such oppressive biblical understanding forming me, I was largely successful in keeping my transgender situation under wraps throughout childhood and adolescence. I didn't mind being a boy at all, and

still don't. I'm not transsexual or intersexual (although I certainly respect and value my sisters and brothers who are), and I don't hate my
masculinity. I genuinely like being a biological male and have never
wanted to change that. Also, I'm well aware of the privilege that comes
with being male in this society. I know I have benefited greatly from
it throughout my life.

However, at times my seemingly unfathomable desires for feminine
expression would become overwhelming. Those desires would well
up inside me in a powerful, inexplicable way. I would then indulge
in the occasional session of cross-dressing, with the predictable result
of creating ambivalent emotions about what I was actually doing. I
knew this much: I was joyful when I was furtively able to dress in my
mother's or sister's clothing, thoroughly appreciating and delighting
in the socially forbidden trappings of femininity. I did all this in isolated secrecy, loving the sensations and enjoying the mental images of
myself as a girl even though there were twinges of guilt at the same
time. Cross-dressing somehow made feelings of self-fulfillment, exhil-
aration, and a unique sense of calmness and inner peace available to
me in a way that was lacking in other areas of my life. It just felt right.
I was whole and happy at such moments, even while questioning the
"correctness" and morality of my behavior.

Looking into the mirror and seeing a girl smiling back was
curiously satisfying, even enchanting, in a strange and almost incomprehensible way. The ancient mystery of transcending gender was
being manifested before my eyes and within my soul. I was captivated by it, filled with awe at the inscrutability and the wonder of
it all. Now, many years later, I still feel exactly the same way every
time it happens.

I remember one day in particular, a time that my mother vividly
recalled years later when I finally came out to her as transgender. I
was somewhere around the age of thirteen or fourteen. My dad, mom,
and siblings had gone somewhere and left me alone in the house.
This happy event created an opportunity for me to experiment with
makeup, something I'd never done before. As soon as they pulled
out of the driveway I locked all the outside doors to the house and
ran to the bathroom, where I immediately dove headlong into my

mother's cosmetics. I spent the next hour or so trying on foundation, eye shadow, eyeliner, lipstick, blush, etc. Of course, I had no real idea of what I was doing (applying makeup wasn't a skill I'd ever had an opportunity to pursue before), but it was definitely exciting to see the way I looked. It gave me a thrill to know that I was doing what girls all over the world did every day, and I was having a wonderful time experimenting with all the different cosmetics. I'd never fully realized how makeup could alter one's visage, and I was captivated by the changes in my facial appearance.

Suddenly I heard a pounding on the front door. My heart immediately leaped into my throat, for I realized I'd lost track of the time and my family had returned. I yelled, "Just a minute!" while frantically trying to wipe off the makeup so I could unlock the door for them. (That's when I learned that makeup doesn't come off too easily with only a washcloth — which, I discovered later in life, is apparently why God invented cold cream, baby wipes, and eye makeup remover pads.) In any case, the pounding on the door grew louder and more insistent. I felt sick, but knew I had to go open it. As soon as I did, my mom took one look at me and knew something was up. "What's that all over your face?" she asked. Trying to appear nonchalant about the whole thing, I replied, "Oh, I was just fooling around. I'm getting it off right now." Not much more was said about that incident, and I considered myself extremely fortunate to have gotten away with little more than a question or two. My mother, however, remembered the episode and brought it up to me many years later when I came out to her, saying, "Now it all makes more sense to me. We wondered what you were up to, and now I know."

Trying to keep my secret was difficult for me. I always felt twinges of spiritual guilt about my cross-dressing, even while I was enjoying the activity itself. The guilt was present, at least in part, because I felt I had to be secretive when I cross-dressed. Eventually I convinced myself that I was behaving sinfully in the eyes of God by rebelling against the teachings of my highly conservative religious belief system. I had already been indoctrinated into the unyielding sex/gender assumptions of my Southern Baptist culture, so corresponding remorse and shame easily became a part of my psyche.

The struggle to make sense of my internalized transgender dilemma went on for over three decades. Honestly convinced that the act of cross-dressing (or even possessing a sense of innate femininity) was sinful, I'd fervently promise God that I wouldn't cross-dress or give in to my feminine desires ever again, and I would always keep that promise — until the next time. My feelings would build up to the point that I simply *had* to dress or else I felt I'd explode. Afterward the religious guilt would come back and even increase. It became a recurring cycle of building desire, cathartic experience, and almost immediate remorse. *Why was I so weak,* I kept asking myself? Was it a lack of faith, of spirituality, of belief, of worth on my part that made me unable to stop having those forbidden and sinful desires?

I'm aware that it must be rather difficult for those who have not experienced this particular type of gender stress to relate to such feelings, but I can assure you that the emotional currents of transgenderism are extremely powerful. For such readers it may be helpful to know that "People generally associate crossdressing with sex, but mature crossdressers emphasize that it is gender-oriented. It is the female social role that attracts."[1] And it attracts vigorously. I can attest to the strength of that attraction. Please keep in mind, though, that cross-dressing is not primarily about sexual gratification for most of us. It's about the power of gender expression.

In any case, the impact of my religious guilt and attendant shame was overwhelming. I became increasingly convinced that I was somehow fatally flawed, corrupt, depraved, evil, and that I was an abomination to God for wanting to wear a dress or otherwise indulge my feminine desires. (Of course, the idea of questioning whether these cross-dressing activities actually did anyone any harm never entered my head. I was far too busy being consumed with all that religiously imposed shame and guilt.) My biblical literalist interpretation of Deuteronomy 22:5 continued to loom in the forefront of my consciousness, indicting me on the old legalistic, fundamentalist theological grounds and causing a great deal of ongoing internal stress.

Theologian Rita Nakashima Brock evokes vivid memories of my fundamentalist childhood when she writes: "Theological systems that carry a longing for an unreal past tend to prohibit our honest grounding in and real acceptance of our life experiences. Such systems of longing are based in nostalgia, the nostalgia of abused children, an abuse epidemic in patriarchal culture."[2] No doubt Brock refers to literal physical and sexual abuse, which research has shown to be more widespread in rigidly androcentric contexts than anywhere else. But there is little question that my church's and family's patriarchal Southern Baptist belief system, while giving me a solid though perhaps rather elementary foundation in biblical knowledge, was also highly abusive in many ways. The rigid biblical interpretations and religion-based gender expectations of fundamentalism forced me to deny an important, even formative component of who I was as a human being. Shame was the result. Consequently, I spent years attempting to hide and repress that essential element of my God-given personality, to the detriment of my psychological, emotional, and spiritual health.

Growing into puberty and then arriving at adulthood only served to intensify my innate desires for transgender expression. The feelings and desires didn't go away as I entered physical maturity; if anything, they grew stronger. I've since learned that such deep-seated emotions rarely fade with age for gender-variant people, but in most cases actually tend to intensify and crystallize as one grows older. Because of that corresponding increase in transgender desire, the socially and religiously induced feelings of shame and guilt may tend to multiply as well.

DECISIONS AND GROWTH

We can repress the truth about ourselves for only so long. Truth makes its presence felt in one way or another. As Leyla Kokmen writes: "In time, as is usually the case, the truth grew restless. It wanted recognition. It began to shove its way through the tiniest cracks."[3]

In my thirties I made a choice that proved to be perhaps the most significant of my life. I finally admitted my own truth to God and to myself: I was gender-variant, although I also confessed I had no idea why this mysterious situation was present in my life or what it all meant. Over the next several years I struggled fervently and honestly to put my gender issue into a workable perspective, particularly on a spiritual plane. I felt that I *had* to know whether God truly did condemn me and consider me an abomination, or whether I had somehow been misled and misinformed about my transgender status before my creator.

This evaluative process eventually led me into a spiritual crucible, my own dark night of the soul. It became an intense time of spiritual self-assessment and reevaluation. That process permitted me to make some life-altering discoveries about myself and my relationship to the God who created me. It was an experience that literature calls "the initiation." Indeed, I was being initiated into a new understanding of my life as a transgender Christian. My experience paralleled that of author Chuck Lofy in that my new insights and discoveries "shook the very pillars of my mind and reshaped my theology and my basic understanding of life. But before that could happen, I had to empty myself of all that I had held as truth. Until then I had seen God as 'out there,' but I began to understand with brilliant clarity that God is also 'in here,' within the human heart."[4] For me, that new awareness was the beginning of wisdom.

I began to seek out books by theologians who wrote from various points across the religious spectrum, with many differing views on issues of faith. I certainly didn't agree with everything I read (and still don't), but it was refreshing to know that I wasn't the only one who was questioning the legitimacy and practicality of fundamentalism and its authoritarian, legalistic approach to spiritual matters. To my surprise and eventual delight I started to realize that there were more humane and inclusive ways to interpret Scripture, to reflect faithfully upon God and creation, to think about issues of sex and gender, to view alternative methods of spiritual self-expression, and to consider my personal transgender situation in the light of my Christianity.

My fundamentalist upbringing hadn't prepared me for such remarkable and spiritually liberating realizations. I slowly became aware that the old belief system which once offered a form of comfort and a seemingly reasonable sense of religious direction wasn't working too well for me anymore. I determined that many of my untenable, outdated beliefs would have to be revamped, transformed, or even discarded completely so I could operate in a healthier spiritual manner. I began to discern that there just might be other (and perhaps even better) answers to the internal struggles that I had endured for as long as I could remember, better and more truthful answers than a fundamentalist religious paradigm could supply. Honest Christian theological questioning and healthy skepticism — what radical concepts for a previously dyed-in-the-wool (and now recovering) Southern Baptist!

Through all this I never really questioned my belief in Jesus as the human embodiment of God's love. I have always known somewhere in my soul that the love of God dwells within me. To be sure, my fundamentalist upbringing scarred me in many ways, but I did manage to receive a working knowledge of the love of Jesus from the Sunday school days of my youth, an awareness for which I will always be grateful. I am also pleased to say that my belief in God's limitless love for me and for all of humankind is stronger today than it's ever been. I have experienced that amazing love throughout my own life, and I have witnessed it in the lives of others. In *The Psychology of Redemption*, Oswald Chambers wrote, "Faith is the indefinable certainty of God behind everything and is the one thing that the spirit of God makes clearer and clearer as we go on."[5] My faith in the creator of the universe continues to grow even as my spiritual consciousness continues to be raised. I am thankful to the one who never gave up on me, but who continues to love, accept, and welcome me as a member of the family.

It helped to learn that I was not the only person in the world who was struggling with such complex issues. Through my research I discovered that there are literally millions of people on this earth who are transgender, many of them Christians who confront the same type of gender-based spiritual conflicts that I'd experienced all my life. Transgender persons have apparently been around since the dawn of humanity, and a significant percentage of the human population appears to be gender-variant to some degree.[6]

However, at that time (the late 1980s and early 1990s) there was nothing of substance or value being published specifically for or about the spiritual needs of transgender Christians. I viewed this as a definite problem. I'd already learned I wasn't the only gender-variant Christian, so it seemed logical that there ought to be at least a few resources available for people who sought spiritual help in such cases. Unfortunately, searching for such resources turned up nothing of significance that could help in the quest for specific meaning and affirmation in terms of my transgender spirituality.

Humbly and fearfully, and with a profound sense of my own limitations, I resolved to try to do something about that disturbing lack of information. I began to feel the call of God to do some work that might make a difference, and I attempted to be faithful to that increasingly evident calling in my life. Some of the best advice I've ever received is to be careful when you feel as though God might be speaking to your spirit and calling you to do something special, for most people simply don't struggle with issues like that. If you believe you're being called, pay close attention and try hard to discern where God may be leading you.[7] I've learned that if you're truly willing to be used of God, opportunities for service will assuredly present themselves, usually in ways you never expected!

WANTING TO HELP

In 2000 I wrote the manuscript for a book that eventually became *Crossing Over: Liberating the Transgender Christian*, an attempt to begin the development of a transgender-based theology of liberation. The publication of that book and its subsequent nomination for a 2002 Lambda Literary award (an award for which Virginia's book *Omnigender* was also nominated and went on to win) was an indicator to me that the legitimacy of our claims as the beloved gender-variant people of God is beginning to be recognized and taken seriously, at least within some areas of society. I'm discovering that a variety of people in both the transgender community and the larger Christian church are receptive and even eager for more information and resources that address the spiritual concerns of gender-variant Christians.

Historically, oppressed minority groups have used their experiences and the truth of their lives to help create their own theologies of liberation. These theologies speak directly to and about their specific issues and struggles. Through a spiritualized understanding of those struggles, people come to meet and know God in many different ways. From such liberative efforts have sprung wonderful advances in Christian understandings of ministry and mission for the world. Transgender people need theological resources that speak to our particular life concerns as well, and in *Crossing Over* I outlined and discussed a liberation theology that addresses the unique spiritual realities and distinctive experiences of our gender-variant lives. As mentioned earlier, the book you hold in your hands is intended to be a continuation and further exploration/development of that theme of transgender theological liberation.

I've been greatly blessed to have my writing published. It's an encouragement to know that others feel I may have something worthwhile to say. I have come to believe that something of a cultural shift is taking place at this moment in history, an encouraging movement involving at least some willingness on the part of the public to learn more about transgender issues as they affect society. Toward that end, I am currently writing a new book about transgender in the workplace. This new manuscript does not deal specifically with spiritual concerns. In fact, it is primarily intended for a secular audience: business organizations throughout corporate America. However, it seems obvious to me that if we choose to actively nurture our spirituality it will manifest itself in every area of our lives, including the part that spends many hours each day in our workplaces.

OTHER OUTREACH EFFORTS

Since 1991 I have been involved in preaching, public speaking, and other forms of educational outreach on behalf of the gender-variant community, with an emphasis on encouraging dialogue around the topic of transgender Christian spirituality. God continues to provide various opportunities for me to share a message of hope and liberation for transgender persons, and I have been fortunate enough to offer presentations and speeches to many colleges, universities, scientific organizations, professional and business organizations, churches, seminaries, and other groups.

I truly enjoy opportunities to speak and share with audiences, and these experiences have been memorable for me. Some of my most meaningful sharing experiences have come through an ongoing involvement with the University of Minnesota's Program in Human Sexuality as a facilitator in their series of transgender AIDS/HIV prevention seminars directed specifically toward the gender-variant community. Such marvelous opportunities for in-depth, substantive discussions and interactions with so many people have been a blessing.

In November 2001 I was invited to be part of a national transgender consultation sponsored by the United Church of Christ at their headquarters in Cleveland, Ohio. This historic occasion marked the first time that a mainstream Christian denomination had ever sponsored such an event, and I was both humbled and proud to be a participant. Approximately a dozen transgender people — lay and clergy, from all parts of the country — met in Cleveland to share our stories and discuss potential strategies for ministry within the UCC. It was a remarkable opportunity to learn from each other, to contribute our ideas, to cry and rejoice and sing and pray together, and to see firsthand what God can do through the lives, ministry, and witness of gender-variant Christians. We met with the Reverend John Thomas, general minister and president of the UCC, and two of his national staff members to share our spiritual concerns. Their warm, compassionate, and affirming response to our personal stories was extremely moving. It will be exciting to see how ministry to the transgender community develops as the overall level of awareness with regard to gender-variant spiritual concerns continues to be raised within the Christian church.

The prospects for spiritual outreach, healing, education, communication, and reconciliation are incredible, but an immense amount of work remains to be done. The cavalier dismissal of gender-variant lives by society and its institutions, including organized religion, is dehumanizing, unjust, and intolerable. We must work now to change that destructive, demonic paradigm if the Christian church is to operate with integrity toward all people as an extension of the love of our creator.

I'm very eager to see what happens next, for God is obviously doing a new thing. I'm excited to be a small part of this adventure. I'm also discovering that being involved in the fledgling movement for transgender justice within the church is a bit like riding a roller coaster: it's simultaneously exhilarating and terrifying. However, as usual (and especially within religious circles), anything new is generally looked upon with much suspicion and misgiving, so I would humbly request your prayers that the work of creating justice might be accomplished in this sacred, innovative endeavor.

Chapter 5

WHAT DOES IT MEAN TO WALK A TRANSGENDER CHRISTIAN PATHWAY?

☿ TRANSGENDERISTS COME in such a dazzling variety of types that it is difficult to define any simple center. The huge contrast between Virginia's life as a "masculine" lesbian woman and Vanessa's life as a cross-dressing husband and father only begins to illustrate the variety within the transgender community. Yet both of us maintain our ties to Christianity and work primarily within — and reaching out from — Christian churches. We believe that transgender Christians need to know that hope and opportunity are indeed possible for us even within the church, an institution that has usually been somewhat less than welcoming toward those of us with gender differences.

Here's some good news to begin with: God loves gender-variant persons faithfully and unequivocally, accepting and welcoming us freely and fully into the family of believers just as we are. This fact has nothing to do with our individual merits or demerits, but with God's loving outreach toward us and energy within us. God has chosen each of us to embody unique aspects of the Godhead within our gender and other particularities. No earthly human being, no organization, no religion, no denomination, no authority figure, and no oppressive system of belief can ever take from us God's presence within us.

As Catholic theologian Catherine Mowry LaCugna has explained in *God for Us: The Trinity and Christian Life:* "Not through its own merit but through God's election from all eternity (Eph. 1:3–14), humanity has been made a partner in the divine dance. Everything comes from God, and everything returns to God, through Christ in the Spirit.... This is what Jesus prayed for in the high priestly prayer in John's gospel (John 17:20–21)."[1] A church faithful to Scripture would therefore never try to exclude anyone who responds to God's love from the full enjoyment of that divine and human communing of mutuality, reciprocity, and equality.

Unfortunately, however, we who care about gender justice must be continually vigilant and ever mindful of the dark, antihuman forces of oppression aligned against us within the institution of Christianity itself. There are exclusivist, legalistic factions within the church that would actively deny our right to exist; to live whole and healthy transgender lives; to come into our full, God-given potential as gender-variant people; and to be equal, contributing members of the body of Christ.

However, we're by nature no alarmists or harbingers of doom. In fact, we're highly optimistic about the future, believing that the day will come when transgender persons are fully accepted within an enlightened society and within its institutions, including the Christian church; a day when God's inclusive welcome is known and experienced by all people; a day when God's will is done "on earth as it is in heaven."

Try, if you will, to reimagine the Christian church operating healthily and effectively in a world that embraces and welcomes benign human difference rather than fearing or shunning it. Christine Smith writes about such a world when she says, "Re-imagining is about discerning and celebrating what is possible: the possibility of a world where no one has the power to dismiss, no one sits while others kneel, no community eats exclusively from the table. It is about the possibility of a world where all people are heard."[2] Now, *that* would be a world worth living in!

However, we're also realists. We try to be pragmatic about these things. We're well aware of the dangers of ignoring or underestimating our ideological opponents, those who fearfully bluster and loudly deny our God-given right to be both authentically Christian and gender-variant. Our road to justice and eventual acceptance will not be smooth or easy. Those aligned against us are seeing to that.

Nevertheless, we ask you to join us in considering what it means to be a gender-variant Christian, one who chooses to remain and make a difference within a church that has historically chosen to ignore and condemn us, often consigning us to invisibility and spiritual starvation so that we are forced to lick up the crumbs falling to the floor beneath the table of God's bounteous feast of communion.

STARTING WHERE WE FIND OURSELVES

"Friedrich Nietzsche once wrote that, 'A person has no ears for that to which experience has given him no access.' In other words, we learn something new only relative to something we already understand."[3] It's admittedly difficult for most of us to accept something as truth if we have no personal frame of reference for it.

Most people don't know much, if anything, about the realities of transgender lives, and what they do know is usually wrong, misinformed, or corrupted by the negative sensationalism of tabloids such as the *National Enquirer* and television talk shows like *Jerry Springer*. That's why we're convinced that if we can begin finding ways to increase Christian awareness of our transgender presence and our actual numbers we can create a tremendous positive difference for the church: in the socioreligious perceptions of who and what we are, in the church's attitudes and actions toward "outsiders," in the church's ability to learn and grow, and in the church's capacity to do justice for all human beings. In such a transformed, renewed, "different" church we can begin to realize and experience the astounding promise that God holds out before us: the promise of abundant life and overflowing blessings to those who engage in the difficult but necessary work of doing justice, creating right relationships, and making peace in this world.

Of course, all of this is much easier said than done. Confronting fear and ignorance by telling our stories and living out the truth of our transgender lives may be a risky endeavor. As the late Steve Allen wrote, many of us "like to quote a statement attributed to Jesus, 'Ye shall know the truth and the truth shall make you free,' [but] when actually confronted with new truths a good many of us tend not only to run away from them but to pause just long enough in our intellectual flight to give the truth-teller a good sound pummeling."[4] After all, killing the messenger is an ancient tradition. Remember what happened to Jesus, who was crucified? John the Baptist, whose head was severed from his body? The apostle Paul, who was also beheaded? St. Joan of Arc, who was burned at the stake for (among other things) being a female-to-male cross-dresser? Mahatma Gandhi, Martin Luther King Jr., and Archbishop Oscar Romero, all of whom were brought down by bullets from assassins? Peacemakers, prophets, and justice seekers don't always have an easy road or meet a peaceful end.

Conflict is never an easy proposition. It's often painful, and no one truly welcomes or invites it. But through our experiences of conflict we may discover, perhaps to our surprise, that our intellect, beliefs, and moral values can sharpen, focus, coalesce, and be understood more strongly and more clearly than ever. Conflict can serve as a tool for making us more conscious, more aware, and more certain of our relationship to God and ourselves, and that's ultimately a good thing — even though it may not be much fun when we're actually going through the conflict itself.

Making a difference in the world is usually an untidy, uneven proposition at best, but if we don't make the effort, transgender Christians will never achieve the equality we need and deserve within the institutional church, the place that is our rightful spiritual home and our heritage. Every journey must start somewhere, and we would suggest that the logical starting point for this journey is in our collective hearts, minds, and spirits.

THE INTERNAL WORK

Our path of discovery will invariably lead us to examine the geography, the uniquely constructed architecture, of our own internal, sacred space. Transgender Christians need to know what we believe about God and why we believe it. We need to know who we really are in relationship to our firstborn brother, Jesus, and then we need to articulate our beliefs passionately, yet lovingly and with integrity, as we live out the truth of our lives. By doing this inner work, and by simultaneously supporting and learning from the inner work of others, we can withstand and ultimately overcome the unjust attacks, untruths, and oppressive ideologies of sociopolitical extremism from the religious right.

The spirit that inhabits, energizes, and directs us is the spirit of God. God put it there, and that divine spirit animates us in remarkable ways. As we journey through life, the spirit inexorably draws us ever closer to God and our fellow creatures, pulling at us, tenderly persuading us, gently nudging us but never coercing us. God doesn't force people to do anything, but always lovingly attempts to influence us to return to the light, to health, to our source, to our essence, to wisdom, and to the divine relational basis of our being.

Our resolve to pursue spiritual and social liberation on behalf of all people must continue to grow, because the determination of those who would oppress us also escalates in direct proportion to their irrational fear of change and difference. Too often our churches are more interested in pursuing conventionality and agreement than in seeking truth, peace, and justice. Indeed, socioreligious conservatism always seems to flourish whenever it can identify a specific enemy. Unfortunately, gay, lesbian, bisexual, and transgender persons appear to fill the role of "enemy," and we have historically been attacked and victimized as a result. Bearing false witness against us has raised huge amounts of money. Transgender people have been easy targets up until now, but we must learn to rise above our victimization by finding new ways to stand firmly and proudly against the irrational fear and negativity of people who vehemently hate and demonize us. We must refuse to live as victims any longer.

However, we cannot afford to live with an attitude of hatred toward those who would destroy us. Instead we must make the decision to love them and keep on loving them until they can't hate anymore. A reciprocity of hate only serves to lower us and make us less than we might otherwise be. Hate keeps us from becoming people who value love and right relationship over all else. Our theme and our goals must always be those of creating justice, a God-breathed justice rooted in the tenets of liberation: liberation in our theology, liberation into the fullness of life, liberation into the mainstream of the church and society, and liberation for all human beings who have been lovingly created in the image of a relational God. Catherine Mowry LaCugna defines what Christian freedom in God's image is all about: it is freedom from sex and gender stereotypes, freedom from "biology as destiny . . . from fear, from compulsions and obsessions, from the need either to dominate or be dominated, free from the cycle of violence, able to encourage the fulfillment of another's happiness and, in the process, to achieve growth."[5]

The Reverend Ken Fox's life provides an excellent example of this kind of liberation. At age eight, Ken knew he was different. When he was twelve or thirteen, he won a Halloween costume contest dressed as a girl and remembers that as a defining moment in his life: "It felt so natural, so real." By his twenties, married and living in Rochester, New York, he felt that something was drastically wrong. During his forties, while he was transforming the Open Door Mission from a one-employee to a forty-employee service for the hungry and homeless, Ken was cross-dressing in secret. But when he was fifty-five, his wife found some of his feminine clothing and confronted him as sinful and shameful. He sought therapy, began to take prescribed female hormones, bought a wig and other accessories, and eventually was able to legally become Kaye Fox. As Kaye, she was denied contact with her six children and seven grandchildren; only Fox's ninety-year-old mother remained supportive. "I lost everything," Kaye says. "But would I do it again? You bet. I'd do it earlier." She is "relieved and happy after years of anxiety,"[6] and that liberation makes the enormous price worthwhile for her. Kaye Fox now lives as the woman she knows herself to be.

Even as we struggle to achieve that blessed gender emancipation while confronting increased opposition, we also ultimately bring about a greater liberation for the rest of the world and for Christianity itself. The church is edified, and God's liberating love is always made manifest whenever any of God's people are able to overcome oppression and achieve peace and joy despite the negative circumstances of their lives. This is one of the paradoxes of being Christian and gender-variant, and it is a paradox that can be useful in teaching the rest of our world about the importance of accepting and embracing difference. Transgender Christians are in a unique position to embody the remarkable freedom of personal, gender-based spiritual liberation, a freedom that springs from the God who created us in such wondrous and mysterious fashion.

Who better than gender-variant Christians to challenge society's binary gender construct, a harmful paradigm which assumes that all "normal" human beings are exclusively either male or female, attracted only to the "opposite" sex/gender, and drawn only to those behaviors, roles, and gender presentations that our society has arbitrarily designated as appropriate to one's genitals? Male-female polarization, in which the female is subordinate to the male, has been sanctified by the right wing of all major religions. Such unjust polarization is ultimately responsible for the feminization of poverty, female infanticide, and other violence against girls and women. Michael Kimmel is surely correct when he argues that "gender *difference* is the product of gender *inequality,* and not the other way around."[7] So as we work to help church and society degender human traits and behaviors and give up gender-based judgmentalism, we are working on behalf of females everywhere. What's more, because permission to lord it over others is a corrupting permission, we are simultaneously working to liberate males from that judgmental prison as well. When we create justice, everyone wins.

THE EXTERNAL WORK

To achieve our liberation as gender-variant Christians, however, we must struggle actively against the unjust, heavily politicized, fear-laden, and white-male-dominated power structures that currently exist. These androcentric power structures are nothing new; in fact, they have held sway within Christianity for many centuries. As Steve Allen wrote,

> When the churches literally ruled society, the human drama encompassed (a) slavery; (b) the cruel subjection of women; (c) the most savage forms of legal punishment; (d) the absurd belief that kings ruled by divine right; (e) the daily imposition of physical

abuse; (f) cold heartlessness for the sufferings of the poor; as well as (g) assorted pogroms ('ethnic cleansing' wars) between rival religions, capital punishment for literally hundreds of offenses, and countless other daily imposed moral outrages. Again it was the free-thinking, challenging work by people of conscience, who almost invariably had to defy the religious and political status quo of their times, that brought us out of such darkness.[8]

Recently, Rita Nakashima Brock pointed out that the idea that Jesus' crucifixion was payment to the Father for our sins emerged most fully during the Crusades, when religion needed a blood atonement theory in order to justify the violent atrocities the Crusaders were being asked to commit.[9] Because violence against women and girls, gender-variant people, and people of other races and religions is still being justified in God's name, the time is right for thinking Christians to defy and transform the cruel and violent status quo.

It's become painfully obvious that the church as an institution is ill equipped to deal with the need for change that our modern world constantly presses upon it. The church typically appears to be mired in the throes of inertia. We need only consider the Roman Catholic clergy's "damage control" difficulties in the wake of the child sexual molestation scandals to understand that the institutional church is reluctant to take swift, effective action on almost any issue, no matter how important or deserving that issue might be. Roman Catholic clergy are not the only ones guilty of abusing children or of hiding behind the power of the church for oppressive purposes.

Theologian Rebecca Ann Parker has said, "It is important to not accept uncritically the traditions of the church and the liturgies, but to engage in transforming them in a more life-supporting way."[10] We find the church fearful, often to the point of paralysis, and thus practically incapable of creating or welcoming significant change on its own. Yet change, the one constant in the universe, is essential if any entity is to grow and mature. For that reason we must literally and lovingly goad the church for its own sake into change, growth, and maturity, for the institution certainly isn't going to change of its own volition. Justice-loving Christians must become willing to enter into the midst of the struggle between churches that have historically and bitterly opposed change and their growing numbers of disenfranchised members, including transgender persons, who demand life-giving change in response to human need. This is a marvelously interesting time to be alive and involved in the struggle. "The stage is set for the most familiar confrontation of modern life — between people who demand change and institutions that resist it."[11]

As we enter this hotly contested theological/social/political arena, we must be acutely aware and forewarned of the intellectual and spiritual dangers of biblical literalism and paradigms of fear. All religions presumably start out with good intent, but most eventually become perverted by fanaticism and misguided zeal; Christianity is no exception. Once any group of people believes it has found the "Absolute Truth," it's a short leap to believing that those who fall outside their particular version of the "Absolute Truth" are somehow unworthy or insufficient. That's how isolationism, convictions of moral superiority, rigid gender roles and behavior expectations, and other cultlike beliefs occur. In Nazi Germany, such a mind-set meant that any person who was not a full-blooded "Aryan" was automatically suspect ... and we all know how that turned out. Many gender-variant people perished in the concentration camps along with the Jews, gypsies, and physically disabled. If the purveyors of authoritarian religion were able to do as they liked, it could happen again. As the eighteenth-century English political philosopher Edmund Burke said, "All that is necessary for evil to triumph is for good people to do nothing."

GATHERING COURAGE TO OPPOSE
DESTRUCTIVE PARADIGMS

Virginia once mentioned to a group of feminists that she is a compliant type who just wants to be liked but has been forced by racial, economic, orientational, and gender injustices to take various unpopular stands. In response, a much younger woman burst into tears and expressed her surprise: "I always thought people like you just *enjoyed* fighting the good fight! It never occurred to me that you had to overcome any fear and reluctance!" We hope that this young woman's realization puts spurs in the sides of her courage so that she too stands up for what she believes to be fair and honorable, regardless of what happens to her popularity ratings. The powerful advance of fundamentalism in the modern world serves as a call to all of us who believe in freedom. We must develop the courage of our convictions in persuasive ways without being coercive.

Fundamentalists of all religions tend to insist that there is only one path, one story, and one author. Any road to God other than the one they espouse is considered false, deceived, wicked, sinful, deviant, heretical, and totally unacceptable. Whether attacking liberal theologians, women's rights activists, civil libertarians, or GLBT folks, and whether they are using purchased radio/television airwaves or hijacked airliners, fundamentalists of all major religions remain convinced that only they are right and everyone else is wrong. That's why some fundamentalists — not all, but many — fall prey to the "end justifies the means" mentality. The events of September 11, 2001, are a prime example of a religious mind-set that seems to flourish within some extremist elements of the Islamic faith, but attitudes eventually leading to such destructive, exclusivist, antihuman paradigms may be quickly and easily found in the fundamentalist camps of all major religions, including Christianity.

For instance, as mentioned earlier, in February 2002 the chief justice of Alabama's Supreme Court justified depriving a lesbian mother of her three children by calling homosexuality "an inherent evil that should not be tolerated: it is abhorrent, immoral, detestable, a crime against nature, and a violation of the laws of nature." This judge went on to argue that the state has the "power to prohibit conduct with physical penalties, such as confinement and even execution. It must use that power to prevent the subverting of children toward this lifestyle, to not encourage a criminal lifestyle."[12] Shades of the Nazis, shades of the Taliban!

Rightwing religious extremists appear to be uninterested, unwilling, or incapable of changing or adapting their beliefs even when presented with a more positive spiritual alternative, apparently because to change somehow implies an admission that their current belief system might also be suspect in some way. Once that possibility is acknowledged, the belief system itself potentially becomes a house of cards and the whole thing could crumble at the slightest provocation. The way to avoid that danger is simply to disallow anything that holds the potential of changing attitudes and behaviors, even if such a change might be for the better. The monolithic belief system then tends to become more important than the individual lives of human beings. People are seen as existing to serve the beliefs, not the other way around. Of course, that way of thinking flies directly in the face of Jesus, who clearly explained (as we've already observed in Mark 2:27) that the sabbath was made for humankind, not humankind for the sabbath. Jesus obviously had his priorities in order, but legalists appear to reject such a profound concept.

Historically, the jump from a belief in the superiority or exclusive truth of one's own religious beliefs to religious totalitarianism, intolerance, and even violence has been very short. Often this myopic mind-set results from the fact that "the criteria by which [people] judge the superiority of their own religion are derived from within the religion itself, thus stacking the deck in their own favor. And all too often, religious exclusivists come to the theologically untenable and morally repugnant conclusion that God would consign others to damnation simply for practicing another faith."[13] This approach is an example of circular reasoning, a highly flawed, pseudointellectual approach to any issue: People maintain an exclusivist belief because their religion tells them to, but the religion has derived that belief from inside itself, thus contaminating the entire process and making it too insular to be any sort of effective, rational argument for legitimate truth. Lest we forget, the idea of Christlike compassion for other human beings really ought to enter in somewhere. That compassionate idea is based not on circular, insulated reasoning, but on the entire Christian Scriptures as well as the accumulated wisdom of humankind.

In right-wing religion, of course, the paradigm of implied spiritual superiority indicates that anyone who is "different" or who doesn't necessarily agree with the religious powers that be must be a "sinner." By extension, it also means that anyone who doesn't fit the conservative/fundamentalist/selective literalist agenda is to be mistrusted and excluded from full and equal membership in the club. Even those rare persons in positions of religious power who may perhaps be philosophically sympathetic to our transgender situation are usually hesitant to voice much support or do anything to make a legitimate difference for gender-variant persons. That's because people in positions of religious power didn't reach those positions by being naïve. They are acutely aware of the inevitable uproar and religio-political backlash that would immediately assail them from the extreme right.

Furthermore, openly "different" people such as the gender-variant usually aren't allowed to participate fully and actively in the life of the faith community, primarily because of fear of possible embarrassment or potential "contamination." So we are labeled as second-class citizens who are fair game for the marginalizing speech and actions of those in the centers of religious power who tend to make the institution's rules and set the agendas. This is a far cry from the loving, respectful, universally inclusive gospel of Jesus Christ, but it's the way power-based, nonrelational religion works, and it's how many followers of such inherently unjust ideologies tend to think and act.

Some of history's greatest spiritual and political leaders — people like Jesus Christ, St. Joan of Arc, Dr. Martin Luther King Jr., and Mohandas K. Gandhi — appeared to be uninterested in acquiring public praise from or gaining institutional power over others. Yet they found that people were attracted to them because they created inspiration by living out a vision far greater than that of personal aggrandizement. Also, they were social or religious radicals who weren't necessarily interested in following oppressive institutional rules, but who cared much more about doing the work of justice than being "acceptable." That kind of human integrity always generates hope, vision, community, inspiration, respect, dignity, mutuality, and vast, exciting new possibilities.

But it is not wise for us to assume that people like Jesus, St. Joan, Dr. King, and Mahatma Gandhi never trembled inside and never cared about what people might think of them or do to them. These people were often angst-ridden over their decisions to put themselves on the line in the cause of justice. We know from Scripture that Jesus felt agony and fear concerning his approaching execution. As Carter Heyward has emphasized, when we dwell on Jesus' power without his openness, or his strength without his vulnerability, we are failing to see Jesus at all.[14] To categorize prophets and activists as totally different from ourselves is in fact a convenient way of excusing ourselves from joining them to do what we can to further the cause of justice in the world.

Our cause is particularly challenging because it involves intimate relationships between men and women. We find it especially painful to think of the many Christian women who are caught up in a form of one-way submission to their husbands, often because their husbands insist upon that as an extension of male privilege. These women have been taught to believe that they are obeying God by allowing their husbands to rule over them, thinking it is God's divine will for them to meekly obey the male instead of developing healthy interpersonal relationships rooted in respect, egalitarianism, and loving reciprocity.

Vanessa remembers the words of the wife of a Promise Keeper (a member of a right-wing U.S. men's group focusing on the "proper, God-ordained, leadership role" of men as "servant-leaders" of their wives). The woman said, "My husband used to make all the decisions in our family. But now that he's a Promise Keeper, we always talk first and then he makes the decision." That's what passes for progressive thinking in some right-wing circles, we guess, and that's the kind of insular, androcentric world that fundamentalists desire: a world where a straight, white, male-dominated hierarchy is firmly in place to control others; a world where "men are men" and women and children are to submit to the whims of their masters; a world where anyone who doesn't subscribe to this gender "norm" is automatically suspect.

Much of the anguish that results from traditional gender attitudes is played out in the privacy of the home, but sometimes the private anguish erupts into acts that become impossible to ignore. For instance, Andrea Yates and her husband were convinced by the conservative Christian culture in which they moved that birth control was wrong, that Andrea belonged at home with the children, that she must provide homeschooling for them, and that her husband should hold dominion over her because she (not he) was derived from the sin of Eve.[15] Convinced that she was a bad mother and that her children would therefore go to hell if she allowed them to reach the age of accountability, Andrea Yates drowned all five of them in the bathtub. Despite her insane reasoning, Andrea was sentenced to life imprisonment while her husband and the misogynistic evangelist who implanted such dreadful ideas in her head are walking free.

Chuck Lofy encapsulates what's going on here when he tells us, "The basic purpose of evil is to perpetuate forms that are self-serving rather than liberating."[16] Promise Keepers, Focus on the Family, the American Family Association, Exodus International, the Christian Coalition, Concerned Women for America, the Family Research Council, and other similar ultraright religious organizations seem to be essentially dedicated to perpetuating self-serving, nonliberative social and religious forms that harm human potential. Such organizations discourage people from experiencing the freedom and joy that spring from developing healthy, mutual relationships with God and each other.

LEARNING TO FEEL WHAT "THE OTHER" FEELS

Transgender Christians and our allies may take heart from the fact that help is arriving from unexpected sources. For instance, the Arts and Entertainment television network recently aired a documentary they called *Role Reversal*, in which two male and two female college students were given three weeks of expert training in dressing, moving, speaking, and acting like the other sex before they were taken out in public to see if they could pass. One male passed as female among women who were buying cosmetics, but became the target of extreme hostility from men ("freak!" "faggot!") who had expressed sexual interest before they realized they were flirting with a male. (Concerning this incident, a gender specialist commented, "People get very angry if they feel you're toying with them and that they have been deceived.")

One female was able to pass as male with about half the audience when she did a nightclub stand-up comedy routine; the other female passed so successfully that she was thought to be male by a group of her own friends whom she was serving in a restaurant. The second male was relatively successful posing as female; a month after the documentary was completed, his mother said that he spends more time with her and seems more sensitive to women's concerns as a result of the experiment.

If ordinary college students can be trained to reverse sex/gender presentations in a mere three weeks' time, obviously men and women are not as "opposite" as traditional society might have us believe. Surely it is an indication that the transgender movement is making significant advances when such experiments are being conceived, carried out, sponsored commercially, and then aired all over the nation. The most encouraging factor of the documentary was the way the students learned new empathy for "the other" through their practice of role reversal. Learning to imagine how other people feel is bound to lead to kinder, more compassionate behavior not only toward the "opposite" sex, but also toward people who are in-between or who may differ in skin color, economic class, age, culture, or physical or mental ability.

Such signs of hope should preserve transgender Christians from despair as we face severe opposition from our fundamentalist sisters and brothers, who may use against us what Dann Hazel called "some of the most hate-filled and insulting rhetoric I have ever heard."[17] We may wonder how people who worship the gentle Jesus can justify engaging in such hateful, insulting speech, but justification is achieved in the same way that all destructive attacks are rationalized: by dehumanizing the person or group we are about to harm. (A missionary once asked a tribe of cannibals how they could bring themselves to kill and eat the human beings in an enemy tribe. The cannibals were extremely surprised by the question, and hastened to explain that it was no problem because the enemy tribe was composed not of human beings, but of animals.) Civilization appears to have done very little to change the barbaric tendency to dehumanize whomever we do not understand and appreciate.

Steve Allen explains, "If the objects of their scorn were perceived as humans, with the same rights (and feelings) as themselves, the haters would be consumed with paroxysms of guilt."[18] Hazel says, concerning the religious right,

> Jesus is their weapon; fear is their tactic. War is the metaphor for their religion. Bringing God to a spiritually starving nation demands the vilification of gays and lesbians [and other "different" groups like bisexuals, intersexuals, and other transgenderists] that, at least in the fundamentalist/evangelical perception, stand in the way of God's great social plan to transform the United States into a New Canaan.[19]

Unfortunately, if you are familiar with the history of the conquest of the biblical land of Canaan, you may recall that a perceived sense of "manifest destiny" encouraged the Israelites to loot, pillage, decimate, and ultimately commit genocide upon the indigenous Canaanite people who were already living in the land. All these acts were, of course, committed under the auspices of alleged instructions from God to "go up and possess the land," thereby deposing the rightful owners and forcibly establishing a nominal theocracy in the name of Jehovah. These actions were justified as being under a perceived "holy" mandate from God "himself," so any cruelties and casualties were justified and blithely written off as collateral damage — the unfortunate but inevitable results of performing "God's will."[20]

The *Women's Bible Commentary* makes clear that although the book of Joshua uses a predominant logic polarizing insiders (Israelites) and outsiders (Canaanites), it also provides several passages that subvert, counteract, and undercut that logic: the messenger of Jehovah in Joshua 5:13–15, for instance, who is neither insider not outsider, but holiness itself. Or Rahab, or the Gibeonites, both outsiders who became insiders.[21] By the time of the prophets, religious understanding had developed to the point that Micah could say that all God requires of anyone is the doing of justice, the loving of mercy, and walking in communion with our creator (Mic. 6:8). Unfortunately, however, many Christians around the world have never paid attention to the biblical movement toward reconciliation, hospitality to the stranger, and compassionate inclusiveness. Instead, "both the Boers of South Africa and the Puritan colonizers of New England saw themselves as a new Israel, led by God to a new Canaan."[22] Acceptance and respect for outsiders was never a hallmark of those particular communities.

Latter-day religious extremists also consider themselves to be the modern equivalent of those ancient Israelites, at least in some respects, and they are quite anxious to take over the United States for Jehovah — "possessing the land," as it were — in much the same way as their Old Testament role models raped and plundered the land of Canaan in the name of their deity. They are convinced that God, in "his" infinite wisdom, has ordained them, the "faithful," to be the chosen leaders of this new theocratic order, and they are highly motivated by a deep-seated religious fervor that assures them of the absolute correctness of their perceived religious mandate. They will stop at nothing to achieve their desired ends, including the exclusion, denigration, and oppression of any who may disagree with or question their agenda, believing that they are "walking in the light," "marching into battle for Jesus," "putting on the armor of God" while engaging in a "holy war against the forces of evil," and thus fulfilling God's "revealed will" through such actions. Human beings ought to be able to do better than that.

We find the idea of any individual or specific group dictating the explicit will of God when it comes to someone else to be alarming, spiritually arrogant, and perhaps even laughable, were it not so dangerous. We trust that any enlightened, rational, and compassionate person, regardless of spiritual background, would feel the same way. Sadly, while some people drink deeply from the fountain of knowledge, others pause there only long enough to gargle.

TRANSGENDER INTEGRITY AND CHURCHLY INTEGRITY

Transgender Christians and our allies may strengthen ourselves by remembering certain basic principles, one of which is that a just and loving God who energizes and flows through all creation would never want us to do terrible things to one another. The four Gospels are filled with stories of Jesus rebuking officials who clung to the strict letter of the law at the expense of love and kindness. In fact, the cardinal insight of all the world's major confessional faiths is that "no religious doctrine or practice can be authentic if it does not lead to practical compassion. Buddhists, Hindus, Taoists, and monotheists all agree that the sacred reality is...enshrined in every single human being, who must, therefore, be treated with absolute honor and respect. Fundamentalist faith...fails this crucial test if it becomes a theology of rage and hatred."[23]

Anything that divides us — anything that causes us to be violent, hateful, or oppressive toward one another — does not originate from God, the author of love and relational power. Whether the issue is racism, classism, sexism, heterosexism, transphobia, ableism, ageism, nationalism, or any of the other ills of society, they all boil down to one problem: a sense of separation from our creator, which in turn causes us to distance ourselves from others on one trumped-up basis or another. For Christians, such identification with *me* and *mine* as opposed to oneness with God and God's creatures is inexcusable. Romans 8:38–39 alone would be enough to demonstrate that truth: "I am convinced," writes Paul, "that neither death, nor life, nor things to come, nor powers, nor height, nor depth, nor anything else in all creation, will be able to separate us from the love of God in Christ Jesus our Lord."

Compassionate men and women of the church are the ones who need to take action toward resolving the many unjust social, political, economic, and religious situations that oppress created beings. We must do this critical work with integrity, commitment, and clarity. After all, as Smith so ably reminds us, "the church's fundamental mission is to proclaim and embody glimpses of the reign [i.e., the kin-dom] of God until such a day and time when all creation will know it fully."[24]

Yet spiritual honesty is sometimes painful, for our cherished traditions and religious mind-sets may potentially be shattered when the truth of reality is laid out plainly for us to witness and examine. We're speaking here, in particular, about the necessity for mounting prophetic challenges to the ultraconservative status quo. Such challenges are tests of our Christian integrity, tests rooted in a compassionate vision of justice, inclusivity, and mutuality for all people. They are powerful challenges that carry the strong weight of moral force against the spiritual immorality of a narrow, rigid, and oppressive pseudo-Christian ethos.

Confronting the power of the status quo is often a daunting and sometimes even a terrifying task. Doing something new and different can easily make us feel isolated, vulnerable, and disoriented. It often precipitates self-doubt and a loss of self-confidence, emphasizing the internal gulf that lies between what we feel we should be and what we fear we might become. However, we — the quiet but overwhelming majority within the body of Christ who would prefer to live in peace, respect, and mutuality with all people of every faith — must pursue with honesty and humility the discovery of divine truth for our lives, knowing all the while that we never can be completely certain about every aspect of God's specific will for ourselves or others.

John Shelby Spong speaks of such integrity when he writes:

> All of our theological disputes and our religious wars through-out history that have been fought over differing versions of the way God is defined represent nothing less than the folly of human thinking. . . . Twenty-first-century Christians must now come to understand that God does not inhabit creeds or theological doctrines shaped with human words. To say these things is not to launch an attack on God; it is rather to state the obvious: that no human words, no human explanations, will ever capture the essence of God.[25]

Given that we finite human beings cannot logically capture God's essence through our words, explanations, or limited abilities of comprehension, we must not put our trust in these things. Instead, we must place our confidence in the existence and the integrity of a God who is indefinable yet very real, intangible yet highly visible in the lives of others and ourselves, and whose divine presence is always manifested whenever we extend love and respect to each other. God is always present in and through our acts of love.

"Honesty will be revealed when the church confronts its world as an institution that admits it does not have all the answers and demonstrates that by a desire to be both a humble listener and a humble learner."[26] Honesty in the church has too often been sacrificed on the altars of convenience, institutional tradition, and the maintenance of an ideology of white male dominion. Honesty is a desired quality rooted in the God-given diversity of human experience, and until honesty takes its rightful place in the hearts, minds, mouths, and actions of church leadership, transgender persons and other oppressed minorities will continue to be unjustly held in contempt by the institutional powers of the church. That attitude of contempt will also continue to control many Christians who sit in certain pews on Sunday mornings, becoming programmed into a mind-set of religious hatred and exclusivity by listening to oppressive rhetoric and hate speech directed toward those of us who may be "different." (It may be useful to remember that presenting only one side of an issue is not teaching, but indoctrination.)

But, thankfully, other Christians are now listening to more reasonable voices: the Reverend Dr. J. Philip Wogaman, former dean of Wesley Theological Seminary, points out that between 30 and 40 percent of the delegates at recent General Conferences object to the United Methodist stand against homosexuality; the most recent Conference explicitly recognized the presence of sincere United Methodists who believe in the just-war theory and equally serious members who are pacifists. Wogaman calls for the church to accept "the virtue of moral compromise," quoting John Wesley's statement that "Every wise man ... will allow others the same liberty of thinking which he desires they should allow him. ... He bears with those who differ from him."[27] That sort of ethical reasoning is good news for transgender Christians and our friends!

Chapter 6

RECLAIMING OUR TERRITORY, MAPPING OUR PATHWAY

⚥ IN SEVEN SHORT VERSES, Mark 1:9–15 relates three major events in the life of Jesus: the baptism, the temptation in the desert, and the launching of Jesus' work as an itinerant teacher, healer, and preacher. The order of events is significant: first Jesus is affirmed as God's offspring, who is beloved, with whom God is well pleased; then come forty days of lonely struggle; and finally Mark writes about the breakthrough of Jesus' "proclaiming the good news of God," which is that the kin-dom of God has come near.[1] Although Mark does not elaborate on what temptation Jesus struggled with, the order of events would suggest that he was wrestling with accepting the privilege and burden of his status as the Beloved Child of God, and therefore as the one who has the responsibility of bringing God's kin-dom near.[2]

We will never know what self-doubts and fears went through Jesus' mind during that long forty days of solitude. But we do, all of us, know the self-doubts and fears that assail us when we hear the news that we too are the beloved children of God, that we too are called to be the carriers of God's peaceful kin-dom into a war-weary world. Those of us who are transgender deal not only with the ordinary self-doubts instilled by growing up in homes that are inevitably less than perfect, but also with cruelties based on the inaccurate binary gender construct. Some of us feel rejected because our bodies are both male and female (i.e., we're intersexual); some of us feel rejected because we are attracted to our own sex rather than to the other sex (i.e., we're gay, lesbian, or bisexual); some of us feel rejected because we seem to ourselves a sex/gender that does not match our physical embodiment (i.e., we're transsexual); and others of us feel rejected because in various other ways we do not or cannot abide by our society's gender roles as assigned to our sex/gender of birth (i.e., we're cross-dressers, heterosexual nonconformists, and/or various other types of transgenderists).

Having struggled not just for forty days but more like forty *years* to accept our status as the beloved transgender children of God, we (Vanessa and Virginia) understand that deep within our minds are vestiges of the cruel judgments we encountered as we were coming to terms with our sex and gender particularities. This chapter is our attempt to root out of our minds the enervating judgments our inner adversary sometimes tempts us to believe just might be true. If we have seemed to focus on the faults of our detractors, our purpose is not to attack them but to understand what makes them tick in order to defuse their power over our minds. In short, as the title indicates, this chapter is about reclaiming our shining transgender identity and mapping at least some of the path by which we can be the purveyors of God's love within and toward the world.

We who are gender-variant are, like all human beings, complex and unique. We are straight, gay, and bisexual cross-dressers; pre-operative, postoperative, and nonoperative transsexuals; intersexuals of many types; drag queens and kings; female and male illusionists; androgynous persons; and other gender outlaws of various kinds. Society considers us to be noncomformists, cultural rebels who some-how manage to transcend, transgress, alter, blur, or confuse the usual categories of gender. To the exasperation of gender traditionalists, we remain human beings who are created in the image of God, which makes us intrinsically valuable and eternally loved by our creator. We are indeed, as the psalmist wrote, "fearfully and wonderfully made" (Ps. 139:14).

Furthermore, the psalmist makes the claim that not only did God form our "inward parts" when we were in the womb, but that God has a book in which "were written down all the days that were formed for me / when none of them as yet existed" (Ps. 139:13, 16). How silly of people to judge one another about things like sexual orientation and gender identity if in fact God formed them within us, and even wrote the details down in an eternal book! Or if, as the Christian Scriptures put it, God "chose us in Christ before the foundation of the world to be holy and blameless ... in love. ... *For we are what [God] has made us*" (Eph. 1:3; 2:10, emphasis ours).

Historically speaking, however, it was believed that most human beings could be assigned to various discrete categories that accounted for cultural, social, sexual, gender, and physical differences. Such theories of human differentiation provided pseudoscientific justifications for claiming racial, sexual, or gender superiorities that resulted in slavery, segregation, apartheid, gay-lesbian-bisexual-transgender bashing, ethnic discrimination, the Nazi holocaust, and South African apartheid, among other occurrences.[3] Our struggle for transgender acceptance and respect is not and never has been against human beings themselves. We're struggling against mistaken ideologies, false scientific/religious assumptions, bigotry and prejudice, and the more divisive elements of human thought and behavior. The fact that such negative, oppressive mind-sets and behaviors continue to be directed toward the gender-variant is the result of many factors, including a plethora of ill-advised legal, social, religious, and cultural expectations, not to mention the weight of history and expediency.

LEARNING TO LIVE WITH AMBIGUITY

A major aspect of reclaiming our own territory as transgender Christians and allies is learning to welcome ambiguity. In fact, research by renowned psychologist Abraham Maslow indicates that human creativity flows from an ability to embrace ambiguity. Discomfort with gender ambiguity is not the exclusive property of conservative people. When Ellen DeGeneres took responses from her audiences during a recent HBO stand-up comedy show, Ellen mistakenly addressed one of her lesbian fans as "Sir." When she was corrected, Ellen smacked her brow and lay down on the platform as an indication of her humiliation at misreading the woman's gender. After the embarrassed laughter and applause died down, the fan tearfully explained to Ellen how much the openness of Ellen and her then-partner Anne Heche had meant to her own life. Ellen signaled the fan to come forward, where Ellen wrapped her in a warm and affirming embrace. That incident provides us with a good metaphor of how to deal with gender ambiguity. All of us, including transgender people, feel insecure about possibly misreading the sex/gender of a person we wish to address. If we make a mistake, we can simply correct it as quickly and lovingly as we can.

Unfortunately, people who are rigid about gender roles and expectations tend to strike out at anyone whom they perceive to be precipitating their own discomfort with ambiguity. As Karen Armstrong puts it, "Many would crave certainty amid the perplexities of modernity; some would project their fears onto imaginary enemies and dream of universal conspiracy."[4] Such persons desperately want to "manifest that lust for certainty which is a reaction to modernity that deliberately leaves questions open and denies the possibility of absolute truth."[5]

"Absolute truth," particularly when it comes to defining who is right and who is wrong about matters of gender and sex, is what some people on the socioreligious right seem to be offering their constituents. Leaders of right-wing religious factions are well aware that "in order to mobilize effectively, a group needs an ideology with a clearly defined enemy."[6] Accordingly, gender-variant people are disdained as scapegoats to be blamed and ridiculed, or else portrayed as powerful enemies who must be fought and eliminated. (It amazes us that people who live in fear of gender ambiguity somehow manage to place transpersons in such radically opposite categories; we're either pitiful scapegoats or powerful enemies, but how can we be both? One would think that we'd be consistently identified with one category or the other, but we usually seem to end up being placed in whatever category best fits the agenda of our oppressors at any given moment.) Transgender persons are repeatedly marginalized so that fundamentalists and other religious right-wingers might transfer their own internal fears onto the "other," thereby bolstering a wounded sense of self-worth and reaffirming the "rightness" of their religious ideology.

All human beings tend to operate from within specific structures in their lives. Theologian/author Chuck Lofy refers to these specific structures as *forms*. He says, "If a person hasn't an adequate sense of personhood, or God's presence, or faith, he or she will naturally become overidentified with form."[7] Fundamentalists often tend to fall into the trap of becoming overidentified with, overvaluing, and sometimes even worshiping form rather than spirit. Lofy tells us, "The heresies of our time are primarily the result of 'absoluting' forms."[8] He goes on to say,

> Those people who do not have self-love, mercy, forgiveness... become overidentified with form. They give themselves away to form. Then, if the form with which they overidentified is taken away, they react destructively. This is why they killed Jesus. Christ tried to separate the Pharisees from an overidentification with law. The paradigm was the law; they had success under the law. Jesus called them hypocrites, living in ego, living in self-satisfaction. They walked past the wounded and knew nothing about healing. They locked the doors to the kingdom [*sic*] of heaven and threw away the keys. "If you were blind, you would not be guilty of sin; but now that you claim you can see, your guilt remains" (John 9:41). There's something other than law, he said. There's love and there's mercy, woundedness, healing — and they killed him.[9]

Saying no to forms and yes to a holy calling is a dangerous thing. It inevitably changes the ways in which we view the world — the church, society, other people, God, and even ourselves. It undoubtedly takes us to new places and shows us things we never imagined. And it may ultimately require great sacrifice from us if we are faithful and if we follow that call with an unwavering commitment. Consider what happened to Jesus, who paid the ultimate sacrifice to follow his calling from God. The calling of the holy, the voice of the sacred, is always insistent but gentle, terrifying but loving, and sacrificial but rewarding. We must learn to pay close attention to the leading of God's call in our lives, for the still, small voice of God speaks volumes if we allow ourselves to hear it.

In the words of his character Macbeth, Shakespeare would probably recognize that modern-day Pharisees are "full of sound and fury, signifying nothing." They can't signify anything of substance because, as a rule, extremist religion does not lend itself to a healthy spirituality. Fundamentalism is a rigid, legalistic distortion of spirit. It's a perversion of religion that allows precious little room for the Spirit of God to dance, breathe, move, bring change and transformation, or engender spiritual creativity and right relationship between people. Fundamentalism is one of Lofy's "heresies of our time," a heresy that absolutizes and worships form to the exclusion of spirit.

Real spirituality, Lofy explains, "involves being so centered in the spirit that one sees the dance of forms. The church today is not what it was fifty years ago. People who have spirit can dance about that. People who don't have a spiritual sense see it as a great catastrophe."[10] It's telling (and tragic) that many evangelicals and fundamentalists view change and new ideas — such as welcoming and affirming gender-variant persons — as dangerous, devastating, and calamitous. Unfortunately, some churches and church leaders would rather die than change. But, says Christine Smith, those who care about peace and justice must take heart, for "a resurrection spirituality will not let go of us and will not allow us to hide behind our comfortable theology at the expense of human life and human justice."[11] The spirit of God is moving and will not rest until justice is eventually created for all people. In the midst of our struggles it may be helpful to remember that salvation and right relationship are always found in the spirit, not in the form, so the spirit is where we must always place our trust.

As mentioned previously, sometimes the overwhelming craving for perceived socioreligious security results in an effort to portray transgender, lesbian, gay, bisexual, and other minority communities as enormously powerful, politically compelling, and financially robust. The latter is especially ludicrous, for if most GLBT persons were that wealthy, do you think we'd have so many problems gaining widespread acceptance and respect in such a materialistic society? People on the religious right usually imagine us, their perceived enemies, to be modern-day barbarians howling at the gates of civilization, attempting to destroy ethics, morality, social structure, and all that "God's people" hold dear. In their fear, fundamentalists tend to use capital letters when referring to these supposed forces of darkness and chaos, using political catchphrases such as the "Liberal Church," the "Gay Agenda," the "Secular Humanists,"the "Homosexual Lobby," the "Militant Feminists," and so forth.

Having a reasonable discussion with people who are engrossed in vilifying your cause and making you out to be the sworn enemy of God and society is difficult. That's why so little rational, constructive dialogue ever actually occurs around these issues between people at opposite ends of the spiritual spectrum. Mutuality-based dialogue, rooted in respect for those who may differ with one's personal opinion, does not appear to be a primary interest or tactic of the religious right. Such dialogue is an important tool for transgender people to possess, and we can always practice mutual respect when we're having an argument with our spouses, partners, or friends. There is no better way for us to learn to live with ambiguity than to hold our peace and speak gently but firmly even in response to what feels like a vile misrepresentation.

Lofy offers a reason for those people who manifest fearful and unfavorable reactions to change:

> Change is a separation from the form. Change separates spirit from form. The more of my spirit I have [invested] in that form, the more I am going to resist change. If I'm really hooked into the form, when adverse information comes my way, I won't even see or hear that information. I'll just manage to shut it out. If new information filters through and begins to pull me apart, I will become angry. I am connected to this, and someone or something is trying to separate me from it. The more force that accompanies the outside influence, the more resistant I become. My first reaction is denial; the second is anger. As new information comes in, I might try to negotiate, make concessions so as not to separate. And if the call to separation continues, I may even go into rage.[12]

For that reason, we need to recognize that true justice for gender-variant people can only come within a social context of right (that is, mutual and reciprocal) relationships. Such favorable associations are effective models of God's desired plan for respectful, beneficial human interaction. While civil rights for transgender people is obviously an important concern for many reasons, laws alone never solve a society's deeper problems; attitudes must change as well, and attitudes are often even more intractable than laws. Justice and right relationship are the paths to peace on this earth, but genuine peace is possible only when all people can hold a respected place within society, thereby allowing us to honor and celebrate our differences as well as our commonalities. Given that we cannot change other people directly, we must live into this future we desire by teaching ourselves the vital lessons of respectful dialogue and acceptance of ambiguity.

Underlying our attempts to speak to one another with mutual respect and to abide certain ambiguities is the decision to live our lives with compassion and loving kindness as our core values. Contrary to the easy-come, easy-go, highly emotional definitions of "love" in American pop culture, to live lovingly is a decision we must make, a decision not only to *will* goodness toward others, but also to *do* goodness toward them. Such a commitment may sound easy enough, but on a daily basis we often become snagged on our own separate agendas, becoming impatient if others don't serve what we imagine to be our own best interests. Deciding to love and then living love are difficult self-disciplines.

But how worthwhile that self-discipline is! It is a tried-and-true psychological principle that "what we give is what we get," or as the popular saying puts it, "What goes around, comes around." Jesus alluded to this principle when he counseled us not to judge so that we would not be judged: "the measure you give will be the measure you get" (Matt. 7:2). Fortunately, the principle works just as strongly in positive as well as negative ways. When we learn to love someone, we widen the circle of goodness to include that person; the wider the circle of our reconciliation and communion with others, the more spiritually rich and powerful we ourselves become. Any "sacrifices" involved in the discipline of living lovingly are certain to yield profound returns.

In saying all this we are agreeing with conservative newspaper columnist Katherine Kersten, who has emphasized that "Love is not a matter of fate or chance, but a decision. . . . It is within our power to create a new definition of love. This love, whose essence is self-giving, does not make our [own] happiness its immediate goal. In the long run, however, it is the form of love most likely to produce enduring happiness."[13]

We are agreeing with Kersten not because she is a conservative, but because on this particular matter she has aligned herself with Jesus as well as with many other deeply wise leaders from many ancient traditions. For instance, speaking about the loss of his homeland and his political authority when he was forced to leave Tibet, the Dalai Lama has said that in the face of such stupendous loss, "You are still a human being, within the human community. You share that bond. And that human bond is enough to give rise to a sense of worth and dignity. That bond can become a source of consolation in the event that you lose everything else."[14] Because the Dalai Lama has drawn his circle of compassionate love large enough to include global creaturehood, he is never away from home, no matter where his refugee status may take him.

Love is truly the most powerful force in the universe. Because God has created us in love and for love, Christians must make the conscious decision to emulate God's loving actions and attitudes in our behavior toward others. Because love is eternal, love will eventually transform everything into itself; we may as well open ourselves to its power now, freely accept God's gift, and determine to share it with others. As a remarkable side benefit, loving others as God has loved us will result in an incredibly interesting journey, one filled with amazing possibilities for living extraordinary lives of service and witness to the world.

No one ever said that the journey would be easy, though. We aren't talking about a walk in the park. Still, God has promised to strengthen and sustain us as we move forward into a future that is rich with possibilities. We must learn to lean heavily upon that promise, for we will need it to hold us up when we grow weak and falter, as we inevitably will. The Reverend Dr. Martin Luther King Jr. once said, "One knows deep down within there is something in the very structure of the cosmos that will ultimately bring about fulfillment and the triumph of that which is right. And this is the only thing that can keep one going in difficult periods." That "something in the very structure of the cosmos" is the presence of a loving, divine Spirit that will help us persist in the difficult yet eminently worthy work of spiritual self-assessment, loving others, and the creation of justice.

TAKING RESPONSIBILITY FOR OUR OWN PERCEPTIONS

Basic to the decision to live a life of justice-love is shouldering responsibility for our own attitudes, moods, and perceptions, rather than blaming external circumstances for them. In their important book on marketing, *The New Positioning,* Jack Trout and Steve Rivkin have written, "We tend to perceive the things that relate to our preexisting interests and attitudes — either to support them or to refute them. People also have a tendency to misperceive and misinterpret communications according to those beliefs. Thus, every listener tends to hear his or her own message."[15] What is true about advertising is intensified when the messages refer to religious belief systems. Jesus illustrated this tendency by alluding to the wood he had worked as a boy alongside his carpenter father: "Why do you see the speck [of sawdust] in your neighbor's eye, but do not notice the log in your own eye? Or how can you say to your neighbor, 'Let me take the speck out of your eye,' while the log is in your own eye?" (Matt. 7:3–4). Reminding ourselves of the human tendency to project our own faults and feelings onto someone else ("transference," in Freudian terms) and then taking responsibility for our own perceptions is one way we transgender people can remain calm in the face of prevailing falsehoods concerning those who are "different."

Transgender people often feel stunned and overwhelmed by the strength of the cultural disapproval that surrounds their lives; we are not suggesting that anyone should internalize that disapproval and give up on living authentically. Instead, we hope it will be helpful to look briefly at how gender rigidity developed and became so widespread that people can indulge in it without ever realizing how much they are nevertheless responsible for their own attitudes.

First, we must be aware that "all cultures are historically contingent and invented. None are objective and natural."[16] Therefore, if we are to better understand the heavily polarized dynamic that exists between the religious right and transgender persons, we must look at the cultural and psychological construct of the "other" as a historical/social/religious/political force operant within the larger society.

As Michael J. Mazza tells us:

> in situations where some form of difference — differences in gender, ethnicity, sexuality, national origin, religious background, etc. — exists between two or more groups, that difference can be turned into a tool by which one group is privileged over others. The privileged, or dominant group, may enjoy numerical superiority, access to greater weapons technology, economic power, or greater political prestige; these or other factors may enable them to maintain a position of dominance. Those groups which are "pushed to the margins" — denied political rights, stripped of their land, or even targeted for mass murder — are often defined as inferior or deviant by the ideologues of the dominant group.[17]

Arlene Stein adds further insight:

> We conceptualize the world into those who deserve inclusion and those who do not. Boundaries mark the social territories of human relations, signaling who ought to be admitted and who excluded. The desire to root out others in order to consolidate a sense of self seems universal. How do human beings perceive one another as belonging to the same group while at the same time rejecting human beings whom they perceive as belonging to another group? Why must we affirm ourselves by excluding others?[18]

In other words, why must define ourselves and build ourselves up at the expense of someone else? Isn't the world big enough — and aren't God's blessings universal enough — for all of us?

Furthermore, "Sociologists tell us that in order to create a sense of social order, which all societies must establish, deviants are created and punished."[19] Toward that end, "Whenever a boundary line becomes blurred, the group members may single out and label as deviant someone whose behavior had previously gone unnoticed."[20] These "deviants" are separated from the normative group and are given a name; once identified and labeled they are more easily perceived as dangers to the group. There is great power in naming something, and Robert Scott and Jack Douglas tell us that the act of naming things that are dangerous demonstrates to those in the community "just how awesome its powers really are."[21] In this way society clarifies what is acceptable and what is not, which group belongs in the community and which is to be excluded.[22]

Of course, we must keep in mind that

> over the centuries, religious communities have been both a haven for hatred and a sanctuary for justice. They have been the place from which some of the most virulent, oppressive justification for evil has come. And they have been the source of hope and inspiration for countless justice-seekers. One need only recall those [religious people] who burned witches at the stake [as opposed to] those [religious persons] who marched in Selma for racial and economic justice.[23]

Virginia finds in her own experience plenty of evidence that religion has been for her both oppressive and liberating. In the Plymouth Brethren assembly of her youth, she was taught that Jesus loves every person; when in her teens religious people told her a different story, she half believed them for only a few desperate years before that earlier affirmation began to reassert itself. Similarly, although she learned exceedingly negative biblical interpretations concerning women's gender roles and the status of homosexuals and other transgenderists, nevertheless she was grounded in a solid knowledge of biblical narratives and principles. That knowledge sprang into new significance when she learned a liberating method of interpreting Scripture, her primary role model being the seventeenth-century Puritan poet and theologian, John Milton, the author of *Paradise Lost*.

For her, as for the world at large, religion has been both trash and treasure.

Vanessa, too, remembers the damaging stereotypical versions of gender roles and expectations that she learned from the rigid Southern Baptist belief system of her youth. However, she also remembers hearing that Jesus did indeed love everyone (which presumably included her). From that hearing she developed a belief in God's love that has never left her, allowing her to maintain a strong faith despite the persistence of religio-cultural attacks on her transgender identity. Like Virginia, Vanessa became grounded in a rich, edifying knowledge of biblical narrative and godly principles. She also developed a great love for the Christian church, a love that continues to this day. When in her adult years she discovered that there were liberating ways to read and interpret scripture, she recognized that religion in her life has ironically been both a curse and a blessing, a spiritual prison and a new world of spiritual freedom.

We should not feel too surprised to hear that a factor that holds such enormous liberative potential can have an equally enormous potential for devastation. Everything of value in human experience can be perverted into something destructive: love, sex, money, possessions, ambition, food, physical fitness, you name it. The greater the potential for good, the greater the potential for evil. Scripture symbolizes this dynamic by using the serpent as both the worst and the best. Although many of us think of the serpent as negative because of its role in the Garden of Eden, we should also bear in mind that a brass serpent on a pole was the source of salvation for those who were bitten by fiery serpents in the wilderness (Num. 21:6–9). In turn, John's Gospel makes the brass serpent a type that points toward Jesus' crucifixion as the source of salvation (John 3:14–15). We mention these scriptural points to encourage those of us who have been wounded by religion to overcome our religious allergies long enough to perhaps to take another look, this time focusing on the liberating theology that will affirm and deepen our spirits.

Fear, too, can be both positive and negative, as Smith points out:

Fear is a powerful and strange thing in our lives. It prompts us to seek protection in times of very real danger. It motivates us into needed changes and surprising adventures. It serves as constant reminder that we are fragile, limited, human. [But] in contrast to these life-giving impulses of fear, we know fear can also immobilize us, cause us to "lock the doors" of our lives, and run away from life into places of isolated hiding. Very few human emotions are as strong as fear. Very few experiences are as overwhelming and disorienting as those moments in life when we feel truly afraid.[24]

Surely we ought to extend a great deal of sorrow and compassion toward those who are so frightened of our benign transgender difference that they must react with violent extremism, hatred, and fear. Much prayer for people who live in terror of the "other" appears to be in order.

Prejudice always springs from ignorance, and fear of the unknown is what gives power to ignorance and its accompanying rhetoric. That's why legitimate, nonsensationalistic education on complex topics such as gender and sexuality is indispensable if Christians are to overcome and move beyond their socially fostered and culturally instilled projections. The church needs to be boldly confronted with the truth and the reality of the lives of gender-variant Christians. Hence our coming out as openly transgender is necessary for the church, for society, and for us as individuals. When people are informed and educated about an issue, and when they can put a human face on that issue, somehow fear seems to dissipate. The strong negative emotional reactions are muted, beneficial conversations can occur, respect can flourish, and reason can begin to hold sway.

RECOGNIZING THAT WE *ARE* THE CHURCH

Another major aspect of reclaiming our territory and mapping our pathway is to deal with the realization that we ourselves *are* the church. In her excellent first novel, *Bethlehem Road*,[25] Nancy Crowe has provided an intriguing update of the Old Testament story of Ruth and Naomi. The protagonist, Ruth, is a lesbian who has decided never again to have anything to do with organized religion because of the hostility she has met therein. At one point she muses, "Maybe there were a few isolated places on the planet where you could sing, in a room full of people, about God's love and know that there would be no qualifiers or conditions tacked on down the line, but she doubted it." To which a multitude of transgender people might well respond, "Amen!"

Fortunately, Nancy Crowe also includes in her novel a Presbyterian pastor who is warmly accepting of diversity. In this way Crowe indicates that not all Christians are alike. That fact was emphasized and further developed by the Reverend Michael Cobbler at the ordination of Anita C. Hill to the Christian ministry. Speaking to an exceedingly diverse audience, Cobber said,

> We are the Church! . . . Because we are the church, we gather in joy and not fear, in hope and not trepidation. We gather in truth and not in falsehood, we gather in solidarity and not in division, because we are, in fact, the Church. . . . The last time I checked, the grace of God shuts out no one! The last time I checked, Jesus was in the house blessing and healing, and there weren't any regulations. Jesus didn't make any prohibitions. So I delight today that our witness is a reflection of opening up the Church, letting heaven shine in and that particularly it is not being done by the usual suspects! It is being done by people who love God and know that a way needs to be made.[26]

Cobbler's words and ideas reverberate deeply within us: "We gather in joy and not fear, . . . truth and not falsehood, . . . the grace of God shuts no one out, . . . Jesus didn't make any prohibitions." It is inspirational and profoundly moving to read such words of hope and opportunity for Christians and for the global church of Jesus Christ. The Reverend Anita C. Hill, too, was apparently thinking along the same lines when she said during the same occasion, "Pastor Mel White of Soulforce said that the Spirit appears amongst the community when[ever] justice is being done."[27]

Cobbler, Hill, and White are correct: God's Spirit does indeed move among us, in us, and through us whenever we take action to create justice. That's why the struggle for the inclusion of all people within the Christian church is so vital to the integrity of that institution. If Christians can't find a way to make the welcoming gospel of Jesus Christ become a reality for *everyone,* then the church loses what shrinking credibility it has, becoming nothing more than a fraud and an anachronism.

The Christian church was never intended to be a private country club that only a select few may join and from which others may be arbitrarily blackballed, excluded, or ostracized. The church is the spiritual home of the family of God, and no one has the right to exclude any person — ANY person — who honestly desires to dwell in that home and be an equal part of that family. Anyone who has a problem with that should ponder John 3:16, especially the part that tells us, "*whosoever* believeth in [Jesus, the Christ] shall not perish, but have eternal life." There are no arbitrary qualifiers, no membership rules, no bylaws, no hoops to jump through, no selection committees, no church boards, no systemic requirements for membership approval within the family of God. There is only the relational love of our creator — pure, uncontaminated, comprehensive, all-encompassing, unconditional, inclusive love — offered freely and openly to any and all who will accept it.

BECOMING THE PROPHETIC, LIBERATING CHURCH

Mapping our transgender pathway takes us one step beyond claiming the church as part of our identity. It is also necessary for us to lift up our prophetic and liberating voices in order to transform the church into the place of joy and freedom it was meant to be. But if the church is to become that place of joy and freedom, it must move beyond its irrational fear of "the other."

The institutional church fears acknowledging that gender-variant persons have been serving and continue to serve the church exceedingly well in terms of membership, ministry, and leadership. Any of you actively involved with a mainline denominational Christian church of any size can rest assured that you already know people who are transgender. You may not know who they are, but you *do* know them. And you'd probably be very surprised by the numbers of gender-variant persons who are functioning in positions of strong, competent, lay and ordained leadership in our churches at this very moment.

Most national and international churches are frightened of admitting that their historic bias against sex/gender minorities is unfounded and cruel. That's why they continue to "table the issue," to "study the matter further," to "wait until the time is right," to "hold off until the climate is more socially favorable," or to ignore us completely, rendering us invisible, keeping us at arm's length out on the periphery, hoping all the while that we'll go away or remain silent rather than force the church to confront its internal prejudices and admit its injustice. We don't need more "ongoing studies" or "discussions of the matter" to determine the fitness of transgender people to be centrally active in the church, because we're already active and involved on every level. What we *do* need is respect and acceptance and love. Most of all we need justice, and we need it *now*. *Justice delayed is justice denied.* To deny justice for gender and sexual minorities even one second longer is to continue opposing God's inclusive love for everyone.

Unfortunately, this unjust, discriminatory attitude toward gender-variant persons, a mind-set rooted in ignorance and fear, has been and remains prevalent within Christendom. In particular, as Bishop Spong has pointed out, "Getting angry, being hostile, acting defensively, and engaging in diverting attacks on extraneous issues"[28] are hallmarks of our detractors' attitudes and behaviors toward those whom they perceive to be "sinful." That is why Christians have a spiritual obligation and social responsibility to transform this unjust situation. The challenge for us all is to do whatever we can to help create the necessary changes. If we value the cause of justice, we can wait no longer to take this prophetic action.

The biblical story of Ruth may provide us with some inspiration as we claim our rightful place as the church and as prophetic liberators *within* the church. As the story begins, Ruth is an outsider religiously, nationally, and economically. But she loves Naomi, and the two of them journey to Bethlehem, where they creatively manipulate difficult circumstances in order to live together and even to have a son. By the end of the story the outsider has become not only a respected insider, but the great-grandmother of King David (Ruth 4:17) and part of the genealogy of Jesus (Matt. 1:5–6). We can't hope to do any better than that! But because we do face a daunting task, it seems wise to spend another chapter devising a theological strategy that may help us move toward the transformation we seek.

Chapter 7

DEVELOPING A THEOLOGY FOR THE TRANSGENDER JOURNEY

A HUMORIST ONCE REMARKED that the seven last words of the Christian church will be these: "We never did it that way before." However, the slowly increasing visibility of Christian transgenderists suggests that sooner or later the church will have no choice but to struggle with the issue of whether or not to welcome and accept us. When the time comes, if the Christian establishment chooses to disregard the just, loving, inclusive teachings and moral practices that Jesus modeled, the church will continue its practice of dehumanizing and oppressing the gender-variant and other minority groups. We will then ask: What kind of Christianity is it that rejects some of God's beloved offspring on such specious, arbitrary grounds as our society's inaccurate construction of gender? If we Christians are going to err, wouldn't it be much better to err on the side of love and inclusion rather than that of bigotry and exclusion? Of affirmation rather than marginalization? Of liberation rather than oppression?

Our calling as transgender Christians is to come out boldly to the church and society whenever possible, to be witnesses of the important truths of our gender-variant lives and experiences, and to make enough righteous noise about our unwarranted predicament that socioreligious exclusionists and fearmongers can no longer shut us up by ignoring our issues or sweeping us under the rug. The church will be forced to confront our concerns and struggle with decisions about what is right, what is just, what is Christlike, and how the institution will deal with us as viable individuals created in God's image. Then, if the church chooses to continue on its arbitrary path of injustice and exclusion toward those who are "different," its hypocrisy and increasing irrelevance will at least be publicly revealed for what it is. (To see what Jesus thought of the abuse of religion by those in positions of power, read Matt. 23:1–15, 24–28, and 33.)

Indeed, and very sadly, the church already seems unfair and irrelevant to many American young people. Pre-1997, when she was still teaching full-time at a New Jersey state college, Virginia often had students who would bring her newspaper clippings about the latest unjust policies passed by various church conventions or general assemblies. Although the news items had little or nothing to do with course work, and Virginia had never asked for such reports, the students knew she was deeply involved in work with various Christian denominations, and they recognized injustice when they saw it. Virginia has often wished that denominational leaders could overhear the unvarnished opinions of the nation's more spiritual youth, many of whom are committed to justice — including gender justice. To paraphrase Robert Burns, if only God would give church officers the gift of seeing their policies as outsiders see them!

Audacious confrontation with injustice has never been easy. Remember Moses going before Egypt's pharaoh on behalf of the Israelites? Or Esther risking her life to confront the king about his treatment of her people, the Jews? Or Jesus going before the scribes and Pharisees on behalf of the poor and underprivileged? Or Gandhi confronting the British authorities on behalf of the oppressed populace of India? Or Martin Luther King Jr. going before the white racists and their unjust segregationist laws on behalf of African Americans? Or the patrons of the Stonewall Inn, led and inspired by transgender people standing up to the unjust demands of the local police? Or Nelson Mandela confronting the defenders of apartheid in South Africa? Most of these leaders were not received well at the time, but their actions eventually made the world sit up and take notice of their efforts for justice. Then things changed.

We who are alive at this moment are extremely fortunate, for we are allowed to both witness and partake in a remarkable period in human history. We're starting to see an exciting groundswell, a true grassroots movement, a legitimate spiritual revolution for justice that has been slowly but surely gaining momentum within Christianity and the people of its various marginalized communities around the world. Things are getting ready to burst wide open in the church, and it's invigorating to anticipate such a spiritually liberating event.

Dispossessed minorities like the gender-variant are discovering that we've long been the victims of a concerted socioreligious effort to render us invisible, humiliated, silent, and disempowered. Some of us are being awakened to the fact that we don't have to live invisibly, silently, fearfully, or in guilt and shame anymore if we don't choose to do so. We can actually do something about the problem and make a powerful difference by being ourselves, by standing up and speaking out on our own behalf, by courageously making our presence known, by living lives filled with honor and integrity, and by refusing to step timidly aside as the religious powers that be continue to marginalize and oppress our transgender sisters and brothers. Many of us have assumed the humiliating role of victim up until now, but we don't have to remain in that role. We can be much more than victims: through our ongoing struggle for justice we can — and we will — become victors and overcomers. We will become the harbingers of social and religious change, and the world will be a better place for that.

In our unity is our strength

Our detractors would, of course, prefer that we remain ignorant of our immense spiritual power, of our innate ability to be a strong moral force for peace and justice in the church and in the world, and of our sheer numbers. To give us a sense of how many transgender people there are, let's look at Christine E. Gudorf's numbers concerning the two major types of intersexuals. Those who have Kleinfelter's Syndrome (XXY sex chromosomes) and Turner's Syndrome (XO sex chromosomes) number over 5.5 million — as many as the entire population of Finland or El Salvador and twice the population of Uruguay.[1] And that's only two out of the many types of *intersexuality,* let alone all the transsexuals, bisexuals, homosexuals, cross-dressers, and other varieties of transgenderists. The sheer numbers are staggering, and by coming out, we can raise churchly consciousness of those numbers. We can also remind the church of Gudorf's gentle but serious warning: "The moral authority of religions, most directly the moral authority of their teaching on sexual [and gender] behavior, is challenged when the imperatives of the sexual [and gender] teaching appear to be based on mistaken data."[2]

To sidestep change, traditionalists would like us to stay silent, unobtrusive, ashamed, guilty, fearful, disenfranchised, and invisible. They would have us remain divided and isolated from each other, knowing full well that a crushing sense of isolation is the best way to keep any people disorganized and powerless. They would much prefer that we who are transgender (including lesbian, gay, bisexual, or any other perceived "undesirable" minority) be expunged from society — and certainly from the Christian church, an institution they consider to be their private domain. Their concerns with maintaining the old, systemic version of religious purity, unity, and homogeneity at all costs have superseded love and compassion for other human beings in Jesus' name, resulting in oppression and injustice for those whom they disdainfully consider to be outside their designated "pale of righteousness." In fact, "the scornful attitudes [toward gender-variant people] from the holier-than-thou set are evidence that insecure, small minded, and controlling Pharisees are attempting to convince themselves that they are somehow closer to heaven"[3] than anybody else.

In *A Little Handbook on Having a Soul,* the Reverend David Hansen writes, "People with too much religion in them — including preachers — are souls polluted by rules, regulations and religious experiences, which they interpret as norms for everyone. They think they know how every Christian ought to live and what every minister should and shouldn't do. They want to regulate how people think."[4] Unable or unwilling to negotiate the complex currents of modern life, these religious extremists seek refuge in a backwater of cultish-type ideology just as some people seek emotional solace in alcoholism, drug addiction, or other destructive behaviors and mind-sets. They look to a simplistic, spoon-fed, authoritarian form of religion rather than to a dynamic, growing, passionate, and *com*passionate life-giving faith. That's not a healthy spiritual paradigm at all; rather, it's the worship of form over spirit. It's idolatrous in the most basic sense.

As Karen Armstrong writes in her book *The Battle for God:*

> Fundamentalists have gunned down worshippers in a mosque, have killed doctors and nurses who work in abortion clinics, have shot their presidents, and have even toppled a powerful government.... Fundamentalists have no time for democracy, pluralism, religious toleration, peacekeeping, free speech, [questions, ambiguity,] or the separation of church and state. Christian fundamentalists reject the discoveries of biology and physics about the origins of life and insist that the Book of Genesis is scientifically sound in every detail.[5]

Armstrong also states that fundamentalism is essentially a religion of rage, embodying a fury rooted in an "almost ungovernable fear which can only be assuaged by the meticulous preservation of old boundaries, the erection of new barriers, a rigid segregation, and a passionate adherence to the values of tradition."[6]

Interestingly, Armstrong describes fundamentalism as a religion of rage, for rage is a singularly unfocused and imprecise emotion. Deciphering the difference between anger and rage, Chuck Lofy writes,

> Anger is specific, focused. When I'm angry at someone, I'm angry for a specific reason. Rage is global, diffuse.... [If] that rage is experienced by someone who is overidentified with form, who doesn't possess a clear sense of self, and the security of form is removed — *his* money, *her* beauty, *his* health is taken away — somehow s/he is wholly displaced. Then s/he may become violent. The underlying threat is loss of self.[7]

Consequently, the wrath of fundamentalists is quickly incurred whenever they feel their power or self-image to be somehow threatened by the presence, appearance, or behavior of a designated "other."

But when the sense of being threatened is hidden by an overlay of self-righteousness it becomes a sacred duty, a divine mandate, to rid the church and society of potential threats to the desired theocratic way of life. That, of course, means marginalizing or eliminating anyone who might be different or who might pose a challenge to their agenda. This convenient and highly effective method of socio-religious scapegoating has for centuries been adopted by social and religious authorities. It's how the Crusades, the Spanish Inquisition, pogroms, slavery, apartheid, segregation, the oppression of women and sexual/gender minorities, and other such atrocities against human-kind came into existence. The historical landscape teaches us that within the realms of religion or sociology, "ethnic cleansing" is nothing new.

Essentially, we're talking about varying degrees of religious fascism that are frequently cloaked in pious rhetoric, shallow platitudes, and superficial sound-bite theology. Antidiversity campaigns, often based upon slickly packaged and smoothly produced falsehoods about a "highly organized" and "well financed" political movement to obtain "special rights" for GLBT persons, are only the latest incarnation of the historical method of securing power and control over minorities by demonizing and creating hysteria about them. This tactic, of course, smacks of the propaganda campaigns that Adolf Hitler employed to drum up nationalistic hatred in Nazi Germany against Jews, gays, gypsies, and other "undesirable" minority groups, including the gender-variant. Such schemes are based almost exclusively on emotional appeal rather than scientific data or common sense, but they're often highly effective in their appeal to the baser instincts of human beings.

All the political rhetoric about "special rights" for gender and sexual minorities is a smokescreen to create unfounded fear and to keep us from securing the equal human, civil, and religious rights that every person deserves. We don't want or need "special rights." We've never met even one GLBT person who believed or stated that we should have anything resembling "special rights." We want only the same *equal* and legally protected rights as any other citizen: the rights to live and work as we choose, to love and to marry whom we choose, to raise our families and contribute to society as we choose, to pursue happiness and fulfillment as we choose, and to do these things with honor, human dignity, and respect as we live our lives within the context of the larger society. That's not a "Gay Agenda" or a "Liberal

Crusade" or a "plot to overthrow traditional family values"; these are legitimate human needs. They are the inalienable rights that every person deserves. In order to achieve them, we need to understand the development of oppressive theology, and how we can go about developing a liberating theology to take its place.

DEVELOPING CRITICAL AWARENESS

The dynamic chaplain of Harvard University, Peter Gomes, has paraphrased H. L. Mencken on the sorry state of contemporary theological awareness: "One would not lose too much money in underestimating the theological knowledge of the average Christian in the [twenty-first] century."[8] Even watching a few quiz shows is instructive in this regard; where question categories are available, the biblical or religious categories are usually the last to be chosen and seem most readily to stump otherwise crackerjack minds. In fact, the general lack of our society's theological awareness is a tool that extremists have repeatedly and effectively used to reinforce and sustain their specious claims of spiritual superiority and the loveless policies of exclusion.

Let's consider how an exclusionist mind-set has gained such momentum within the church. Situations like this don't happen in a vacuum. Exclusionism is the result of a process that comprises several layers of personal and communal deception. It involves fear, a lust for power, and an insidious methodology that, at least on the surface, appears foolproof and inarguable to the theologically naïve and uninitiated.

Oppressive theology stems to a great extent from the use of selective literalism in biblical interpretation, and particularly the use of that selective literalism as a bludgeoning, legalistic weapon. In actuality, many forms of biblical criticism and scriptural interpretation have become available to those who are unafraid to seek a more scholarly, comprehensive way to consider the Bible's text and messages for humankind. Some of those critical methods of assessment include redaction criticism, historical criticism, text criticism, reader response criticism, form criticism, literary criticism, eschato-logical criticism, dialogue, praxis (or intentional social activity), and corporate versus individual critical approaches. Many laypersons re-main unaware of these various interpretive tools and hermeneutic methodologies, probably because the right tends to attack, down-play, or ignore the significance of biblical analysis as a legitimate aid to spiritual understanding. Right-wing Christianity simply isn't in-terested in reading or experiencing the Bible's messages through a liberative, justice-oriented lens of interpretation.

A valuable primer on how to read the Bible intelligently comes from Grant R. Osborne in *The Hermeneutical Spiral: A Compre-hensive Introduction to Biblical Interpretation.* Although Professor Osborne, his publisher (InterVarsity Press), and the divinity school where he teaches (Trinity Evangelical) are all conservative, Osborne issues precisely the warning that *all* interpreters of the Bible should heed: "The critical interaction between competing systems [of in-terpretation] is essential for a pluralistic approach to truth, for preunderstanding [i.e., one's preconceived notions] makes it quite dif-ficult to identify weak points in one's own system. The criticisms of others highlight those anomalies and enable one to move closer to the text."[9] Osborne goes on to recommend "an attitude of openness to truth" so that we can welcome challenges from other interpretive communities. Their interpretations might turn out to be more cor-rect than our own, or we might both be wrong; at the least, if we are hungry to discover truth, the challenge will drive us deeper into the text.

When an interpretive community insists upon using a selective liter-alist hermeneutic, or interpretative stance, as a tool to "prove" that its particular social paradigm is "godly" and preferential (and therefore not susceptible to argument or honest debate), such a hermeneutic can easily gain a foothold in the minds of people who may be willing to buy into the supposed "stability" of this religious mind-set. The re-sult is often a perceived "unity" of thought and action derived from an enforced "common understanding" of what Scripture says and means. This approach, in turn, can lead to a convenient justification for negative, oppressive, mean-spirited attitudes and actions toward any who may question, disagree, or think differently with regard to that perceived "common understanding" or "unity."[10] When listening to the insistent "truths" being trumpeted by the religious right, we might recall the words of the Quaker leader William Penn: "Truth often suffers more by the heat of its defenders than the arguments of its opposers."

PROOFTEXTERS AND SELECTIVE LITERALISM

Theological prooftexting refers to the act of removing a passage of Scripture from its appropriate social or historical context, then selectively using that passage to justify a particular position on some issue. It's not a fair or just method of theological argument by any means, but the religious right uses prooftexting as a highly successful method for selective biblical interpretation within its faith communities. "The Bible says what it means and means what it says," is a refrain often repeated in right-wing religious culture. If only things were that easy!

The historical record shows that many groups and individuals have used theological prooftexting to make the Scriptures appear to say whatever seemed to serve their best interests at any given time. Oppressive notions such as slavery, misogyny, racial segregation, heterosexism, homophobia, and transgenderphobia have all been supported by those who invoked selected Scripture passages as "proof" of the correctness of their ideologies.

Selective biblical literalists tend to use religious legalism and a narrow, noncomprehensive theological perspective to disguise a lack of genuine involvement and legitimate struggle with complex, modern social/spiritual issues and concerns. According to Gomes, biblical texts used to justify the oppression of gender and sexual minority groups are "historically conditioned and are, in fact, overruled and superceded by the biblical principles of love and charity toward neighbors and enemies as exemplified in the teachings of Jesus. The Bible [cannot and should never] be used to justify actions contrary to the moral law of Christ."[11]

Along the same line Bishop Spong writes that a proper use of the Bible is "not to quote its literal words but rather to look at its underlying principles, which then must be faithfully applied to life's changing circumstances. Those principles are that every human being is holy, created in God's image, and every human being is loved and valued by God in Jesus Christ, and every human being is called into the fullness of life by God's Holy Spirit."[12] Given that our interpretations are always driven by desire — we see what we want to see — it seems apparent that some church members feel no desire to grasp the universal scope of the transcendent, inclusive idea that Jesus Christ's life and message exemplified: The power of love is always stronger than legalism, and inclusive love ultimately wins.

We need to understand what's really going on here. In a sense, we're talking about how the *spirit* of the law must take humane, life-giving precedence over the *letter* of the law. For any Christian person, the compassionate teachings, moral implications, and embodied example of Jesus' love in relation must always supersede religious legalism. If they do not, then that person must, by default, become utterly dependent for religious security upon obeying the vagaries and inconsistencies of humanly interpreted scriptural statutes, hardly a stable or tenable theological position. It's difficult enough to accurately understand all the Bible's laws, much less to keep every one of them!

The religious right has effectively used selective literalist interpretations of Scripture to justify its own ends of power and thought/behavior control over others. It has set aside Christ's overarching example and message of love and acceptance for the dispossessed and the stranger while embracing a calculated effort to achieve a perceived sense of religious unity, thereby further securing its own socioreligious power base. In the end, though, selective biblical literalism fails as a practical or liberative theological tool. It doesn't work because it's an incomplete, inherently faulty system in which to anchor one's understanding of godly principles and the transcendent law of love. Selective literalism fails to take the bigger picture into account, thus sorely limiting the potential of human beings to become all they might be in relationship to God and God's creation.

In 1881, Archibald A. Hodge and Benjamin Warfield published a highly influential defense of biblical literalism in the *Princeton Review*.[13] Their article became a standard for biblical literalists because it outlined the basic tenets of literalism in a way that made sense to many. Hodge and Warfield declared that every story and statement in the Bible was "absolutely errorless and binding for faith and obedience." Anything and everything the Bible mentioned was absolutely "true to the facts." In addition, they set forth the rather unscientific proposition (which was actually more like a presumably unassailable argument) that if the Bible said it was inspired, then it *was* inspired. Their rather naïve theological/scientific position was, of course, a prime example of circular reasoning. "Such a view had no rational objectivity, was closed to any alternative, and coherent only within its own terms."[14] Still, like so many on the far right, Hodge and Warfield simply could not imagine or entertain the idea that any belief that differed from their own might be viable.[15] Gomes informs us that

> literalism is dangerous for two reasons. First, it indulges the reader in the fanciful notion that by virtue of natural intelligence the text is apprehensible and therefore sensible. Despite genuflections to the notion of original or authorial intent, meaning is determined by what the reader takes out of the text, and this meaning the reader attributes to the author. Thus, what the reader thinks is there becomes not merely the reader's opinion, but the will of God, with all the moral consequences and authority that that implies.[16]

Gomes cites the case of Paul Hill, the man who in 1994 shot to death a doctor who performed abortions. Hill committed this murder in Jesus' name, stating that he was performing God's will by eradicating evil.

Gomes continues, "The second danger of biblical literalism is that the power of private judgment may well obscure the meaning of a text by paying attention only to what it says. Literalism thinks that it is freeing the text from layers of early Christian antiquity and medieval exegesis."[17] As Gomes points out, literalists imagine that if they avoid allegorical, typological, or symbolic interpretations, they are able to preach the Word of God without any corruption of literary devices. What such interpreters do not realize, however, is that literalism itself is part of the eighteenth-century illusion that truth and meaning are identical, fixed, and discernable to reason and common sense.[18]

According to Gomes, then, the selective biblical literalist stands in grave danger of allowing personal conceits and opinions to cloud the meaning(s) of the text by either consciously or unconsciously imposing his or her own interpretation upon it. In addition, the selectively literalist reader is effectively deprived of the rich, transcendent mysteries and continually evolving new meanings and insights that Scripture offers to humankind.

READING CONTEXTUALLY

There is certainly nothing wrong with using the faculties of reason and common sense, but when dealing with issues of spiritual complexity we must also depend upon other informative, influential elements. If we are to make good decisions about issues of spiritual consequence for our lives, we need:

- the guidance of the Holy Spirit
- the witness of Scripture
- consideration of church traditions
- the accumulated knowledge and wisdom of humankind
- our own personal imaginations and experiences

Selective biblical literalism, to its detriment, discounts or minimizes these important additional factors.

The dangers of basing an entire theological doctrine or an ethical judgment on one or even a handful of individualized, selective, and literally interpreted Scripture texts can be illustrated by considering Paul's apparent endorsement, found in 1 Corinthians 7:1, of the notion that "it is good for a man not to touch a woman." Taken out of its original context, this verse of Scripture could easily be construed as a warning against heterosexual marital relations, an idea that most religious conservatives would find appalling. However, Paul's words are there in black and white. Do these words in 1 Corinthians really "mean what they say and say what they mean," or is there more going on here than we might imagine at first glance?

Or suppose a list were compiled of Genesis 9:20–27, Leviticus 25:44–46, Colossians 3:22, Colossians 4:1, Ephesians 6:5–9, and Titus 2:9–10. Do you think such a noncontextual compilation of Scripture verses might provide a sufficient argument for biblical literalists to support slavery? In fact, for several centuries, it did just that. However, most of us understand and would freely admit that, despite these disparate biblical references, slavery runs counter to the very revealed nature of God. As we can readily observe, a grave danger arises when anyone appropriates selected Scripture verses and interprets them in a literalistic manner to further an oppressive agenda.

The sheer selectivity of theological prooftexting is demonstrated by several fundamentalist authors who forever prohibit male same-sex acts by lifting Leviticus 18:22 and 20:13 out of their context in the Holiness Code, but who claim that it is now quite acceptable for married couples to have intercourse during the wife's menstrual period. Yet the latter practice is prohibited in the very same two chapters as the former, Leviticus 18 and 20! The authors justify their upholding one prohibition and canceling the other on the basis of new scientific understanding of body fluids, acting as if none of the research concerning homosexuality has any relevance whatsoever.[19]

Or take the passage that has caused so much grief to Christian transgenderists, Deuteronomy 22:5: "A woman shall not wear a man's apparel, nor shall a man put on a woman's garment, for whoever does such things is abhorrent to the Lord your God." Removed from its historical context as part of Israel's Holiness Code, this passage seems a clear prohibition for all people in all places and all times. But when we consider the context of biblical Israel, another — and quite different — perspective appears. Those people felt that pollution occurred whenever two or more things were mixed that seemingly did not belong together — fabric mixing several kinds of fibers, males supposedly "acting like women" by having sex with other men, human beings having sex with animals, different animal species mating together, planting several kinds of seed in the same field, cross-dressing,[20] or making love with a menstruating woman and thus confusing several different functions of her body. Depending on the circumstances, our culture no longer considers the mixing of kinds to be necessarily polluting, as witness hybrid roses, permanent-press fabrics, or multigrained cereals.

When read in context, what appears to be a clear and universal prohibition against cross-dressing in Deuteronomy 22:5 turns out to be closely tied to ancient Israel's understanding of "mixtures" that seemed to them a disturbance of "the harmony of the cosmos."[21] To that should be added the very real concern in ancient Israel that the people were to strictly avoid any practice similar to the cross-dressing worship of several goddesses in rival cults. Such avoidance was considered essential in order to establish the difference between Israel and the surrounding cultures.[22] Therefore, just as Vanessa commented in chapter 4, the biblical prohibition of cross-dressing is applicable only to that specific time and for those specific purposes.

The above examples illustrate some of the problems associated with taking certain parts of the Bible literally and quoting selective passages of Scripture out of context to make a point without fully considering their historical, social, religious, and ethical implications. In short, it's pretty easy to make the Bible say anything you want if you choose to appropriate a passage out of context and apply it selectively. The purveyors of this approach almost always fail to recognize the more important and overriding principles of God that are found in the Bible, principles such as justice-love overcoming the attitudes and actions of hatred, exclusivity, bigotry, prejudice, and unfounded bias.

Cross-dressing author Lacey Leigh makes justifiable fun of the misappropriation of selected Scripture passages for oppressive ends:

> Farther along in [Deuteronomy 22] are such delightful tidbits as: 22:11, 'You shall not wear a material mixed of wool and linen together' and 22:12, 'You shall make yourself tassels on the four corners of your garment with which you cover yourself.' Not to mention the classic in 22:21 in which a bride found

not to be a virgin shall be stoned to death or that pesky reference in 22:30 to a " ...father's skirt... "? So until those who
are condemning cross-dressing [or other benign transgender be-
haviors/presentations] begin keeping kosher and wearing four
tassels on single fibre garments, I'll just assume that they are
simply using the Bible as a justification for their raw prejudice
and bigotry.[23]

In other words, if you're going to attack others as sinners on biblical
grounds, it might be wise to be consistent in your interpretation of
the Scriptures. Not only that, but if you're going to assume the task
of judging others, you should probably be above reproach in your
own life.

The message of the gospel is for everyone, and any religious rules
that arbitrarily keep people from coming to God or being included in
God's family should be ignored or abolished. One tries (and usually
fails) to fathom the motivation for such exclusivist measures, for at
the very heart of the Christian faith is the knowledge that life itself,
and all its myriad joys, sorrows, opportunities, and responsibilities,
are sacred gifts from a loving God, gifts that are freely offered to all
people.

TURNING DREAMS INTO REALITY

So what does all this mean for us who are both transgender and Christian? First, as Paul reminds us in Ephesians 6:12, it means we aren't
struggling against flesh and blood. The enemy is not people, not our
human sisters and brothers, although it may seem or feel that way at
times. No, our enemy is *evil itself,* the subversive egocentricity that de-
stroys human spirits and fosters hatred and division between people
who are created in the image of God. As the Reverend Dr. Rembert S. Truluck reminds us, "The enemy is [often] within ourselves in
the form of idolatry, ignorance, fear, hate, anger, discord, disputes,
greed, and the other works of the flesh ('human works') referred to
in Galatians 5:19–21."[24] The enemy is often manifested in a destructive paradigm of lovelessness, an unhealthy pattern of thought that

leads to oppression and injustice. Our enemy is a method of biased, prejudicial thinking that excludes, marginalizes, and oppresses other people in the name of God.

Put another way, our enemies are the unholy, antihuman powers of this world, the forces of malevolence that work their nefarious schemes in the darkness and secrecy of a collective false consciousness. Any one of us can fall prey to that false consciousness, simply by setting up our separate egos as innocent and judging other egos as guilty. The darkness of legalistic judgmentalism always hates the light of forgiving, all-encompassing love. This enemy hates the idea of inclusivity, respect, honor, and acceptance, and of celebrating human difference and God's delightfully created diversity. The good news is that ultimately we can learn to overcome evil with love by striving for the intelligent, compassionate application of Christlike teachings and principles, calling upon the strength of God to sustain us in our difficulties, and learning how to live in respect, mutuality, and reciprocity with all of God's creation.

The next implication for gender-variant Christians is that we must seek each other out. We need to find each other; to come together; to mobilize; to form coalitions with others (both transgender and nontransgender alike); to build strong, loving, inclusive community; and to develop ways of being powerfully effective on our own behalf against the evil of any warped, vicious, soul-killing, exclusivist, evil, pseudoreligious mind-set. We must seek to partner and work closely with others who share our commitment to the struggle against oppression in all its forms, cooperating closely with all those who comprehend the need to think and reflect and take action to create positive change. Together we must develop multiple strategies for achieving our goals of liberation, peace, and justice, because solving the numerous problems that confront gender-variant persons with only one tactic is virtually impossible. We must struggle on many fronts, not just one, because all issues of injustice are inextricably connected and interrelated in what ethnologist Clifford Geertz called "webs of significance."

But why all this emphasis on coming together for a common cause? Why should we work closely with others in doing that? Essentially, the reason is that we can't be nearly as effective when we operate alone. There is strength in numbers and, as we discovered earlier, our numbers are significantly larger than most of us imagine. The sheer number of transgender Christians that we've personally met or heard from over the years is remarkable. There are *many* of us! We may sometimes feel isolated and alone, but believe this: We aren't. When we discover the actual strength of our numbers, we will become a considerable force for good in the world.

There is a Brazilian proverb that says, "When we dream alone, it is only a dream. When we dream together, it is no longer a dream but the beginning of reality."[25] May we join our dreams of transgender spiritual and social liberation into a powerful and collective moral force that creates justice for all people. Living in justice will then no longer be a dream. It will herald the beginning of a new, life-affirming reality for everyone.

Chapter 8

COMING OUT
AS AN ACT OF FAITH

⚧ THE FOLLOWING RESPONSIBILITY or obligation for a Christian who is gender-variant is possibly the most difficult and challenging of all: We must find ways to come out by openly revealing our transgender status to our churches and faith communities, to our friends and loved ones, to ourselves, and to God. Christine Smith says, "Coming out is that process of revealing the fullness of who one is as a [transgender] person to one's family, friends, church, employer. It is the act of making one's identity as [transgender] public."[1]

God made us (Ps. 139:13–14), and we have no secrets from our creator. As we discussed in chapter 2, God already knows all about us. However, it will benefit us greatly to take the actual step of admitting to God — while giving thanks, preferably out loud in prayer and in the presence of others — that we are indeed gender-variant. Through the process of opening up our lives in this manner we may offer our whole selves to the one who created us in love and for love. With this step, we're being honest, and when we live with honesty God blesses us by enriching our lives in ways that we can't even imagine.

As Lee Frances Heller explains, being gender-variant "was not our choice in life. We entered the womb this way and the construction of the body began."[2] A false consciousness stimulated by erroneous social constructs causes us to hate ourselves and think we are offensive to God. Heller continues,

> Does the vase the potter made turn around and ask, "Why have you made me this way?" (Rom. 9:20) No. The clay has to ac-

123

cept the way it has been made into a vase to ever display the
beauty of the flowers put into it. God has given [transgender
people] a beauty of soul that only each individual person pos-
sesses. We are gentle, loving people. We are genuinely caring
people. Our basic nature is inoffensive, plus many other positive
traits.... Everyone, including the mighty bastion of the Church,
has tried to remake us and it can't be done. THEY are the ones
mad at us. Not God.

Heller then draws some obvious conclusions: "Stop pronouncing
judgment on yourselves. ACCEPT the fact that you are made as God
made you."[3] Fortunately for us, when we fall short and become dis-
tressed, we have "a God who is large enough to take our rage, our
confusion, our questions, and perhaps our unbelief, and continue to
love us and hold us close in times of trial and confusion."[4]

But why should we who are gender-variant come out? Why put
ourselves at risk at all? Why should we even consider confronting the
threats of potential rejection, heartache, and hassle by coming out?
To those fair and important questions our answer is manifold. First,
Christians are called to be people of integrity, which means hazarding
the risk of being open and honest with others about who we are.
This comment is not meant to imply that all transgenderists who are
closeted and able to "pass" are lacking in integrity. We do not want
to blame the victim of gender bias any more than we'd blame the
victim of racial bias. As long as our society is willing to countenance
hate crimes and employee firings over gender issues, some people are
at too much risk to be able to come out. Nevertheless, we need to
share the truth of our lives as the transgender people of God as soon
and as often as we possibly can.

Next, the desire to be known is a very human quality. To stifle
or repress that desire is to invite the eventuality of negative consequences. Also, others need to know what kind of people we truly
are so they can learn and grow into their own human possibilities
from the example and inspiration we may provide. In addition, we
must come out so we can actively refuse to remain participants in
our own ongoing oppression, including that of our gender-variant

Christian sisters and brothers along with any other person who is suffering under the weight of injustice or marginalization. Our sense of transgender self-esteem must become stronger than our fears.

Our own empowerment is essential if we are to develop a strong sense of individual and community transgender identity. We affirm this passionate statement we found online:

> When a group of people are still oppressed there's an "ed" attached to their name. For example: The Colored; The Retarded; The Handicapped; The Intersexed; The Transgendered. When [our consciousness of] oppression shifts, the "ed" verb changes into a noun: People of Color; People with Mental Challenges; People with Disabilities; Intersex People; Transgender People.
>
> Stringing Gay, Lesbian, Bisexual together, it's easy to grasp that Transgender-ed is anything but equal status in verb form. Transgender deserves to be a noun. Dropping the afflicted -ed from Transgender helps Gender Supremacists embrace Transgender people as People. Words matter. "What starts as a sound ends in a deed."
>
> Imagine saying, "The Heterosexualed"! "I'm Gayed"? Or, "She's Lesbianed"? Or, "We're Bisexualed"? The poor victimized, the transgendered. Having had something done unto. . . . Simply Transgender. Transgender People. Transgender Person. Transgender Movement. Transgender Studies. Transgender Culture. Transgender Politics. Transgender Theory. Drop the -ed to assume the noun status. Doing so signals the group's empowerment.[5]

We must gather enough strength to pull ourselves up by our own bootstraps or ankle straps, and we must do so because:

1. It's the right and logical thing to do.

2. It's a matter of simple justice.

3. No one else is going to do it for us. We have to take on the responsibility for creating change ourselves.

4. The actual benefits of coming out and standing up for ourselves are incalculable for the world, for the church, for the
transgender community, and for our individual lives.

INTEGRITY'S QUEST — AND COST

The Reverend Dr. William R. Johnson has written, "The quest for
integrity is the ongoing process of integrating the components of
self into a congruent, meaningful whole. Affirming our [transgender]
orientation . . . , rather than accepting negative cultural or ecclesiastical
definitions of our identity, is essential to the process of integration."[6]
A flood of new biological and psychological evidence about transgenderism makes more keen our responsibility to make public our
rejection of repressive teachings and policies. Our obligation to come
out to the church as transgender is critical if we truly care about
creating justice for ourselves and for all people.

On April 16, 1963, the Reverend Dr. Martin Luther King Jr. wrote
his famous *Letter from Birmingham City Jail*. In that letter, King
wrote eloquently of the need for taking action and refusing to sit
back passively any longer in the pursuit of justice. King addressed
the letter to his fellow clergy, who were criticizing him for pushing
forward with the nonviolent protests of the Civil Rights Movement.
While many black clergy felt that African Americans should be more
patient, King insisted that without the pressure of the protests he was
leading, equal rights for black Americans would never happen.[7] His
words continue to ring true, not only for African Americans but for
transgender persons and any others whose oppression continues to
this day: "We know through painful experience that freedom is never
voluntarily given up by the oppressor; it must be demanded by the
oppressed. . . . There comes a time when the cup of endurance runs
over, and [people] are no longer willing to be plunged into an abyss
of injustice."[8] That's what our coming out as gender-variant persons
is all about: our demand to be taken seriously, to be allowed the
freedom of gender expression that is rightfully ours, to shout aloud
that our cup of endurance is running over, and to stop our plunge into
the abyss of injustice within both the church and the greater society.

We must prepare our hearts, minds, and spirits for the potential stressors that are certain to develop as a result of coming out. In fact, coming out within the church will almost surely precipitate the surfacing of tensions that are already present. Those tensions and underlying gender-based injustices exist, whether we act upon them or not. The existence of injustice creates a moral imperative for us to act, and especially to expose injustice before the light of human conscience. We must not overly concern ourselves with the additional tensions that such exposure might generate, although we must always be respectful of others to the best of our ability. In other words, stress will happen, so accept that fact and do what needs to be done anyway. We must meet those tensions directly, confronting them with the undeniable truth of our transgender lives. Before such a witness, injustice will falter and eventually fail completely.

Now, we're not naïve about the difficulties of coming out. We may be frightened of telling anyone that we have these feelings and needs inside our hearts and deep in our souls. The fear of rejection and retribution is genuine, and sometimes the repercussions can be very real, too. We've been in those shoes and we know about that fear firsthand. We well remember what living in the fear of disclosure did to us. We remember how fear wreaked havoc on our sense of self, on our pride as human beings, and on our understanding of who we truly are in relationship to God. We know, too, that continuing to keep this beautiful, divinely created part of ourselves hidden away while we cower in shame and embarrassment incessantly eats away at our God-given sense of self-worth. Taming the demon of internalized transphobia is a necessity for every gender-variant individual if we are to make progress toward wholeness and a healthy integration of our physical, psychological, emotional, and spiritual elements. Self-realization involves coming out inside; we begin by confronting ourselves, accepting our reality, and dealing with our fears. We can then begin to look outward toward the rest of the world, and there's plenty of transphobia to confront out there.

Pat Conover tells us there is a wide range of positive and negative alternatives to which transgender people may turn in dealing with the personal and socialized experiences of gender incongruity in their lives. These alternatives include (but, because of the innate creativity of transgender persons, are certainly not limited to) denial of the awareness, the feeling, or the stark reality of one's gender-variant status; rationalization of one's feelings about gender incongruity; resisting or avoiding the discomfort caused by one's gender status through reinforcement of the alternative; resisting the exploration of one's gender feelings; exploring "safe" transgender expressions within accepted social boundaries; sublimation of one's transgender feelings; pursuing androgynous alternatives; expressing transgender feelings or interests in a private or socially protected setting; engaging in part-time open transgender expression; making a full-time transition to the other traditional gender; engaging in part- or full-time claiming of a transgender identity; and reducing one's attention to gender roles and just doing what one wants to do.[9] The real trick for any gender-variant person is to avoid the paralysis of fear so we can move ahead in our exploration and eventual understanding of what transgender looks and feels like for each individual. Fear is a natural response to the dangers of potential social reprisal, to be sure, but we can't permit our fear to subdue or limit our human growth.

No one in her or his right mind is thrilled about running the risk of rejection, loss, or retaliation that coming out may precipitate. However, we must understand that God's accepting, unconditional love for us is a deeper and even more powerful reality than our fears. God never promised to take away all our problems, and God didn't say we would never suffer, but God *has* promised to walk beside us and strengthen us through our difficult times. If we go about it with integrity and intelligence, we transgender people can come out to others on our own schedules and in our own ways. From personal experience, we can guarantee this much: the more we come out, the more our lives will be enriched. We will feel very, very good about ourselves as we watch God working in and through us to bring about understanding, enlightenment, respect, and acceptance in others.

Any person who cares about integrity longs to operate from a place of truth, a place of comfort and internal peace. Continuing to keep a masquerade going on in our own lives, especially about something as intrinsically important as our gender orientation, is debilitating and dehumanizing. In addition, it's hard work to hide one's true self. It doesn't feel good because it's a charade and a caricature of our personal truth. There is always a high price to pay (emotionally, psychologically, physically, spiritually) for continually playing all those different roles and pretending to be someone we're not.

Many of us were robbed of the opportunity to experience a happy, healthy transgender childhood. We were forced to adopt a nontransgender role in order to survive, but, as adults, most of us now have the freedom to rethink and actually choose to do something about that incapacitating situation. Do we remain closeted, living in denial because it's what we're used to? Do we stay in the closet because we're too afraid to be real? Are we too afraid or ashamed to admit to others and ourselves that we're gender-variant human beings who are lovingly fashioned in God's image? At those times of self-recrimination we may want to recall the words of the late singer and actress Ethel Waters, who said, "I know I'm somebody, 'cause God don't make no junk." We may be transgender but, like Ms. Waters, God made us — and therefore, we ain't no junk either. Once we have come to that compelling realization, we can begin to live in the power of a full frontal faith.

Much of the emotional difficulty we face in coming out as transgender can be laid at the feet of internalized shame, a condition instilled in us by a gender-polarized society. We are taught to blame ourselves for being "different," and the result of internalizing that negative teaching is shame. We're not talking about feeling bad for something we've done; that's guilt. Guilt is an emotional response to the idea that "I made a mistake." Shame, however is a very different animal. Shame is about the rejection, not of our actions, but of our very selves. Shame is a warped, negative, internal response to who and what we are as human beings. Shame says, "There's something terribly wrong/sick/sinful/evil inside me. I'm worthless. No one, not even God, could love me." Quite often, for gender-variant people, self-destructive behaviors such as drug and alcohol abuse, wanton sexual promiscuity, self-mutilation, and even suicide are the direct result of shame. Shame denies the goodness that is inherently ours because we are created in God's image.

Coming out as transgender can sometimes be a difficult and even frightening prospect, it's true, but it's also the most liberating and beneficial thing we can ever do for ourselves, for other gender-variant people, for society at large, and certainly for the body of Christ. It feels wonderful to be yourself, and the more you do it, the easier it becomes. In our experience, those "worst-case scenarios" we so vividly imagine almost never happen. Unless a person foolishly invites disaster in some way, the odds are good that such disasters simply won't occur. You put yourself on the line to some degree, no question, but the joys of being open and living with honesty and integrity far outweigh the numbing, soul-killing, disempowering, illegitimate, and ultimately false "security" of the closet. As Lacey Leigh says, "Most of the terrible reactions we anticipate are but phantoms of our inner fear. Fear is the tax that conscience pays to guilt, so the solution is simple: lose the guilt and stop allowing others to define you!"[10]

Author Betty Berzon writes about the power of coming out: "Self-disclosure tends to reduce the mystery that people have for one another. In so doing, it facilitates honest communication and builds trust between people. It brings people out of isolation and makes possible understanding of that which was previously perplexing and even frightening."[11] Our suggestion for any transgender person is to come out into the light of honesty and personal truth as soon and as often as you can. That way you can live your life openly and without fear of potential discovery by others. You won't have to worry about possible blackmail any longer. Fear simply can't abide the light of integrity, and fear always flees when that brightest of lights shines upon it.

Vanessa writes:

I can tell you from personal experience that, at least for me, all of the above is true. Over a period of time I have come out as gender-variant to my wife, my children, and my mother, other family members, friends, coworkers, and the owners of the company where I work. No one has rejected or ostracized me, and in every case I have been able to actually strengthen my relationship with them. I have to believe it's because they could see for themselves that I was doing my best to be genuine, respectful, honest, and authentic in terms of my transgender status. It's amazing how powerful the experience of living intentionally and acting with integrity toward self and others can be. I've learned that while closets may be good for storing clothes, they're horrible places for people to live. Closets are dark, close places. You can't breathe or stretch or grow or become or overcome in a closet.

You don't need to come out to everyone all at once, and you don't necessarily have to tell everyone you know, either. Coming out is a lifelong process, a developmental progression that can teach us much about ourselves and others. Want to learn more about the fascinating mysteries of the human condition and human relationships? Just start coming out to others, then observe the dynamics as they ebb and flow in remarkable ways.

It might be helpful to review some testimonials of several other transgender sisters and brothers who have had the courage to come out. *The Secret Wardrobe* is an hour-long documentary about cross-dressing men, mostly heterosexual, which was produced by the MSNBC cable network. The documentary emphasized that cross-dressing is less about sexuality than about personality expression, and it showed the tremendous relief and tenderness these men feel when they are dressed. Even one man who had lost his marriage after coming out said he was glad to have the freedom to be himself by dressing several times a month. Several people stressed that going to transgender clubs, while helpful, is not enough, because these clubs are still a way of operating "in the closet." A cross-dresser from Houston, Texas, described the fact that he'd gradually told everyone in his life about his full nature, including his employer, IBM, with no negative effects. His assessment of transgender life is this: "Real acceptance will come only if people know the truth."

One male-to-female transsexual sent a memo to all the other employees at her workplace just at the time she was gradually changing her appearance by taking hormones. Her memo announced, "I have decided, after careful evaluation and soul-searching, to live full-time as Marlene." Some of the responses she received were enthusiastically supportive, others were lighthearted, and still others focused on the shifting nature of the relationship people had with her. In general, a few responses to transitioning transsexuals are negative, but the overwhelming majority of people offer encouragement and support.[12]

Dann Hazel tells the story of one minister who confronted a conference panel of four lesbian and gay Christian ministers in California, insisting that they could not be saved unless they turned from their evil ways. When the attack ended, one of the panelists revealed that he had been a fraternity brother of the attacker. He reminded the attacker that they had often partied together, that they had loved one another. "I am still the same man I was back then," he continued. "God loved me when you and I were college friends, even though He knew I was gay. Why would God despise something He created? In fact, God and I are closer, now that I am honest."[13] That kind of self-disclosure brings about sex/gender justice; and notice the testimony that accepting oneself and living in open honesty brings one closer to God!

Dr. Fritz Klein and Thomas Schwartz have edited a fascinating book of excerpts from e-mails sent to one another in 1998 and 1999 by married bisexual and gay men. Many of these concern the process and results of coming out. A bisexual man named Mike is fairly typical, writing that "My wife and I are closer now than ever in our 20-plus years together. The openness and courage we've been able to find has strengthened our respect for each other and our selves." And he comments sagely, "In the end, we must all follow our inner wisdom. Trust your*self*. Come out when you feel ready. As one very wise brother on the list once told me, 'Go tell it in your heart... before you go tell it on the mountain.' Self-acceptance is fundamental."[14]

On the strength of these testimonials and our own experience, here are some brief words of advice about coming out as transgender. We don't claim to have all the answers, but we feel these general guidelines work in most cases:

- Please don't jeopardize yourself or others unnecessarily or un-intelligently. Be smart about this. Come out only when it's right and safe for you to do so. Do it when you're ready, but don't wait forever. Life's too short.

- Do your homework. Inform yourself about what it means to be gender-variant, and do your best to understand the nuances of that orientation and its unique manifestation in your own life. Make sure you've educated yourself as much as possible so you can speak to others intelligently, yet simply and honestly, about your transgender situation.

- Rehearse what you want to say and how you want to say it. Make it personal and honest. Tell your own story, and keep it simple. Try not to become too complex with your explanations, but instead depend upon God to guide your conversation. What happens after that — reactions, responses, attitudes, actions, and so forth — is not your responsibility.

- Please don't be obnoxious or overbearing in your behaviors or explanations when coming out. First impressions are critical for acceptance, so try to put yourself in the other person's shoes and act in a way that is appropriate and respectful. The other person is honoring you by listening to your story, so reciprocate by respecting their time and their willingness to hear you out.

- We strongly suggest that you talk to your creator about this issue at length before coming out. Pray with simple honesty, asking for God's help in this important matter. Admit to God that you have these feelings inside you and that you want to deal with them in a truthful way. If you'll sincerely ask God to help, the Holy Spirit will be present to offer you the peace, insight, and direction that you seek.

- Our creator gave us common sense; we're expected to use it, especially in complex, potentially risky situations. Please be careful and wise, but also be courageous. Remember, your life and welfare are important to God, to your transgender sisters and brothers, and to the world.

THE COMING-OUT PROCESS

There are three simple things you need to know and understand about coming out. These are nonnegotiable if one is to be effective in coming out to others:

1. Coming out is a process.

2. You must honor and respect that process.

3. You must know where you are in the process at all times.

Coming out as a gender-variant person is a truly remarkable (and lifelong) procedure. It's an act of faith, certainly, but it's also an act of the heart, conscience, and will. Like most processes it tends to occur in stages, and we now offer for your consideration a five-stage model of coming out.

STAGE 1 — AWARENESS

The first stage of coming out as transgender involves a dawning, even undeniable, internal awareness that one is somehow "different." Feelings of difference and isolation in the early years of life are apparently very common for gender-variant persons. That's because our transgender orientation doesn't seem to line up neatly with the rigid man/woman, masculine/feminine, either/or dichotomized gender expectations that society insists upon and continually reinforces. So this first coming-out stage is mainly about recognizing that we somehow feel "different" inside.

For most of us, that growing awareness seems to spring up naturally as we experience conflicting emotions of confusion, internal complexity, and differentiation from the gender-based social "norm." Those feelings don't diminish with age but, interestingly enough, usually seem to intensify as we grow older, repeatedly and increasingly demanding attention. Almost inevitably they require some sort of specific action to help bring about resolution to our internal experience of gender difference.

STAGE 2 — ACKNOWLEDGMENT

The second stage of transgender coming out is one of recognizing and admitting, first to ourselves and eventually to others, that we are indeed gender-variant. However, not every transgender person comes out to other people. Many of our gender-variant sisters and brothers live closeted lives because of culturally induced shame, ignorance, fear of reprisal, or other factors that prevent honesty and openness about transgender orientation. We grieve for their pain, but our intention is not to judge such persons. As previously stated, we've been there too. We deeply respect individual decisions about such an intensely personal situation. Yet we want to encourage all gender-variant people to come out whenever and wherever possible because the rewards, for both the individual and society, are immense.

Muslims use the word "jihad" to refer to a holy war, a struggle that was intended to be waged with the Koran, not with terrorist activities.[15] For people who are gender-variant, the greatest of all jihads often takes place inside ourselves. Make no mistake: This is indeed a holy war, an internalized, sacred conflict of immense importance and proportion that we're struggling through. It's a powerful encounter between the negative, highly influential forces of a transphobic society and the God-given transgender orientation that exists inside us. Having a strong connection to our inner selves and to the God who created us as gender-variant will help us to be less dependent upon the outer world and/or the opinions of others for approval, affirmation, and acceptance.

Self-actualization can be a daunting experience. It's not necessarily an easy thing to say, "I am transgender," or "I am homosexual," or "I am a cross-dresser," or "I am bisexual," or "I am a transsexual," or "I am intersexual" for the first time. Try saying the appropriate phrase out loud to yourself in front of a mirror. Consider how taking that action sounds and looks and feels to you. Is it difficult to even get the words out? Do you feel silly or foolish? Embarrassed? Ashamed? If so, keep trying until you can say the words aloud without choking on them. It may take awhile, but that's okay. Want to change the way you think and act? Then change the way you speak and the words you use when referring to yourself. Keep reminding yourself that, "with a simple acknowledgment of self and spirit come an incredible freedom and a new balance in life."[16]

Having a great deal of accumulated shame about being gender-variant is not at all unusual, for our society strongly pushes us in that direction anyway. Often we're too ashamed even to admit that we have shame! We must therefore be extremely gentle and compassionate with ourselves. It probably took us many years to reach this point, so things most likely aren't going to fall into place for us instantaneously. Acceptance of a transgender orientation usually happens incrementally and over time, not all at once.

Keep practicing. Developing self-confidence in this area usually requires a concerted, ongoing effort to change an acquired, ingrained cultural mind-set. Have imaginary conversations with yourself and with others, thinking about how you might eventually discuss your gender-variant status with someone else in an open, respectful manner. Consider what you might say and, equally as important, what you probably shouldn't say. Don't get bogged down with too much scientific theory and psychological verbiage — just try to tell your own story as simply and honestly as you can. There's a genuine power in personal narrative, and you can tap into the truth of that power. It's your life, you've lived it, and that gives it automatic credibility. Remember, you have the right to be yourself.

This step is important, so don't dismiss it or overlook it. After all, if you can't learn to accept yourself and speak comfortably about who and what you are, how can you realistically expect others to accept or be comfortable with the circumstances of your transgender situation?

STAGE 3 — RESEARCHING OURSELVES

The third stage in coming out as transgender involves a great deal of exploration and personal discovery. We begin to learn about our gender-variant orientation, the remarkably diverse community to which we belong by default, our transgender situation and identity, perhaps even some transgender history; often there is deep investigation into how we should most effectively manifest, express, and present our gender-variant orientation to the world. For some, this involves various cosmetic or even hormonal and physiological changes. In a relatively small percentage of cases, it may involve sexual reassignment surgery. For others, gender-based exploration may become more of an internally focused and highly spiritual journey.

In any case, this stage of coming out includes a desire to find out more about ourselves and our place in the world. How do we fit in — or not? How can we best express ourselves — or not? Will we live happy, fulfilled lives — or not? Who or what determines our level of happiness as transgender people? What can we do to improve the quality of life for ourselves and other gender-variant persons? All these questions and many more are part of the discovery process that this coming out stage entails. It can be an exciting time of learning, growth, and stretching, taking us into new personal territory while offering the opportunity to become more fully realized as human beings than we ever imagined.

STAGE 4 — MOVING OUTSIDE OURSELVES

The fourth stage of coming out has to do with developing relationships with others, both within and outside the transgender community. This element is a crucial element in helping us first to envision and then to accept ourselves as gender-variant people. We humans were created to be relational. If no one knows we're gender-variant, it's difficult to have a true and healthy relational sense of ourselves as intrinsically worthy human beings who happen to be transgender.

It's also difficult to believe that others would still love us if they knew. Vanessa recalls her own fear and trepidation on the day she came out to her mother. It was very difficult for Vanessa to open up and share something so personal and "out of the ordinary" with her Southern Baptist mother, yet she was convinced that she needed to take that step so as to have a deeper relational integrity with her mom. Fortunately, Vanessa's mother is a wonderful person who allowed the love of God to supersede her traditional religious background. Her Christlike response was, "You are my child, and there is nothing you can do to make me stop loving you." By coming out to her mother Vanessa was able to unload the burden of keeping her "secret" from someone she loves dearly. Now she is able to speak openly with her mother about transgenderism, and one remarkable result of that openness is that Vanessa's mother prays daily for her and for those who read this book, including you. God works in mysterious and wonderful ways!

Virginia remembers her closeted days only too well: when speaking invitations were extended to her, she always wondered whether the inviters knew her true nature. Often she did not dare to ask, so that preparing the presentation felt like balancing on a high wire without a safety net. Nowadays, she simply says, "I presume you know that I'm a transgender lesbian. Will that make any difference to your institution and to the audience?" The response helps to clarify for her whether the invitation should be accepted, or whether it might be better handled by someone else. Therefore, being "out" provides her with a way to save time and energy and to protect herself from contexts that might feel diminishing for no worthwhile purpose.

Most of us find that we need genuine human interaction and personal relationships in order to help our internalized gender-variant selves become more real and definitive in our personal contexts. If we can't have relationships with others who know us as openly transgender, it's almost impossible to think of ourselves as complete people because we're too busy hiding an integral part of who we are. That's never conducive to a healthy self-image or total self-acceptance.

STAGE 5 — INTEGRATION

The fifth and final stage of coming out has to do with combining all the things we've felt, learned, and experienced into a more comprehensive understanding and positive acceptance of ourselves as gender-variant individuals. When we become able to perceive and embrace ourselves as blessed and gifted because we are transgender, we can begin to live our lives in a manner that is conducive to great happiness and fulfillment. We also discover that each of us can be (and probably already are) a contributor and a gift to society, not a detractor or a parasite. We each have much to offer the world simply because we are who we are. We will find that this stage of coming out is a never-ending journey of learning and discovery, always offering remarkable new surprises and insights as we continue to grow in self-awareness and personal understanding.

COMING OUT AS PERSONAL STATEMENT

Coming out has been called an act of love, and it is also an act of faith. It is a compelling proclamation of God's love and acceptance for us as people. Coming out is a powerful declaration about our individual acceptance of that divine love as we, in turn, embody and share the love of God with others.

A positive, openly transgender identity might be described as a visible delivery system, an outward expression of those intrinsic qualities and values that make us gender-variant on the inside. Coming out indicates that we can love others and ourselves enough to be honest about who and what we are. Such honesty celebrates the goodness that dwells within us as God's beloved transgender people. Coming out empowers you and me to show that we are viable, worthy human beings, that we have something good to offer the world, and that we have a rightful place on this earth.

Looked at from a different angle, coming out is an act of love toward God himself/herself/itself. As Peter Shaffer's great play *Amadeus* makes clear, God needed Mozart to make music and thus to be God's flute. Amadeus was a strange, queer, quirky creature, but it was precisely through that personality and those gifts that God sought entry into the world as Wolfgang Amadeus Mozart and his musical legacy. Shamanistic cultures, including various Native American tribes, understood that transgender was not so much a choice as a calling, and for that reason they respected their transgender children and adults as being chosen and called by the Great Spirit. But after hearing all our lives that our gender-variant natures are evil, we find it difficult to recapture the awareness of many other cultures that in fact transgender is a sign of a sacred designation. Yet so it is.

Perhaps reading some transgender history will be helpful in that recapturing. We recommend Leslie Feinberg's *Transgender Warriors: Making History from Joan of Arc to RuPaul* (Boston: Beacon Press, 1996); *Cassell's Encyclopedia of Queer Myth, Symbol, and Spirit* (New York: Cassell, 1997); and chapters 4 through 6 of Virginia's book *Omnigender.* These chapters deal with "Judaism and Christianity on Creation, Crossdressing, and Sexuality," the confrontation of sexual continuism with Scripture and church history, and intercultural and transreligious "Precedents for Increased Gender Fluidity."

Coming out also informs the church that we exist, that we are here, that God is present within us, that we care enough about our faith communities and ourselves to take this important step boldly, and that our spiritual concerns are as important as anyone else's. In addition, coming out forces the church to confront and struggle with its own reactions to our gender-variant presence. Coming out demonstrates to Christianity that transgender people have been and continue to be loyal members of the body of Christ, members who have all along made legitimate, useful contributions to the church. Coming out declares that we love the church enough to take a stand for justice, courageously putting ourselves on the line even in the face of our fear of rejection or potential retribution.

In addition, coming out means we have admitted to God and to ourselves that we are unique individuals who have been blessed with a gender gift, one that gives us fresh insights and unique perspectives into the mysteries of human existence. While it may be a major challenge for some in this polarized, binary-gendered culture to recognize or accept, our transgender status is truly a remarkable blessing that God has graciously bestowed upon us for any number of reasons. That is a sacred, holy thing, and we gender-variant persons must learn to welcome and celebrate this gender gift wholeheartedly. Not only that, but we must learn to invite others to celebrate with us.

FINDING ALLIES

Remember, too, that even though it may sometimes appear as though you're the only one in the world who feels the way you do, you're not alone. You have literally millions of transgender sisters and brothers in the world, and many of them have come out very successfully. More are doing it every day. You can do it, too. There are growing numbers of support groups, therapists, resources, books, referral organizations, and the like that are available to help you as you consider coming out.

Even if you live in an isolated community, you can usually find help via the computer. Use the Internet and a search engine to find some of those sources. For example, go to *www.google.com* and type in the words "transgender resources." (Vanessa writes: *I just did that very thing and found 145,000 results. My guess is that at least some of those web pages can be helpful for you. Try it and see for yourself.*)

You'll be amazed at how much help is available online. Also, try contacting the International Foundation for Gender Education (at *www.ifge.org*) for information about many areas of transgender interest.[17]

Remember, you don't have to go through this coming-out process by yourself. One newer and very exciting development within religion is the increasing number of local churches that are taking steps to do justice work through becoming open and affirming for GLBT persons. The Welcoming Congregation movement, a loose association of various interdenominational efforts on behalf of GLBT people, is growing rapidly within Christianity, and you should learn about it.

Just to give an idea of how *many* Christian/spiritual support groups are available, consider some of them that recently began making concerted efforts toward transgender inclusion: the Universal Fellowship of Metropolitan Community Churches, Lutherans Concerned, Brethren/Mennonite Council for Lesbian and Gay Concerns, Affirmation (United Methodist), Integrity (Episcopal), Dignity (Roman Catholic), Evangelicals Concerned (interdenominational), Presbyterians for Lesbian and Gay Concerns, Kinship International

(Seventh-Day Adventist), National Gay Pentecostal Alliance, and the Kirkridge retreat center in Bangor, Pennsylvania (interdenominational). While we don't advocate any one denomination over another, it's a fact that the United Church of Christ is becoming a leader in recognizing and affirming the validity of transgender spiritual issues. You can contact the UCC Coalition for Lesbian, Gay, Bisexual and Transgender Concerns for further information.[18]

Although the organization is not specifically Christian or religious, the group Parents, Family, and Friends of Lesbians and Gays is a good place to begin when seeking community support. Recent PFLAG newsletters indicate very intentional consciousness-raising efforts concerning specifically transgender issues.[19]

It's important for any Christian, especially those of us who are gender-variant, to find a supportive faith community where we can feel accepted and nurtured. Your whole life shouldn't have to be a battle. Everyone needs a spiritual home where they can be welcomed, loved, and respected for who they are. We pray that you find just such a place where your spirit can be strengthened and where you can be continually reminded and assured of God's unwavering love for you as a transgender person.

You need to know, too, that not everyone in the Christian church is aligned against us. In fact most people, Christian or not, aren't even aware of our significant numbers or our issues and therefore don't care one way or another; they just don't know enough about transgender persons to have an informed opinion. Don't forget, they're seeing through that mirror dimly as well, so we must always afford them the benefit of the doubt. Because millions of Christians are supportive or at least neutral on this issue, we need not feel we'll automatically be condemned by everyone claiming to be a Christian. An increasing number of clergy and congregations are welcoming, affirming, loving, and inclusive, and you may well be able to find support from one or more of them in your area. Pray that God will bring the right people and situations into your life, and you'll be astounded at how they seem to pop up when you least expect them. We've seen it happen time after time.

TAKING PRIDE IN WHO WE ARE

Earlier in this book we mentioned that one of our primary themes was hope. We want to reiterate something for those of us who may be struggling to accept the idea that we can genuinely be both transgender and Christian: Transgender people are human beings, lovingly created in the image of God. Because all humans are the product of divine genetics, we have the right to fully and confidently claim our status as the beloved gender-variant people of an inclusive, accepting creator.

Youtha Hardman-Cromwell writes, "I'm not just a body. I'm not just a spirit. Neither are you. I'm both, a complex integration of physical and spiritual. I'm human. So are you."[20] Her words should ring loud and true for all people, and especially for gender or sexual minorities who recognize in themselves also a complex integration of masculine and feminine. We are all created by a loving God, and that automatically makes us worthy of everything good that life has to offer.

Don't ever allow "religious" people to convince you that you are somehow sinful, worthless, defective, evil, or unlovable because you are transgender. Such persons have a right to their opinion, of course, even if it's wrong — but then, so do you. Don't acquiesce to the fear-based lies of those who would tell you that you can't be a transgender Christian, that you somehow aren't fit to be part of the body of Christ, that because you're gender-variant you're unworthy, that you can't make a difference in the world, or that you're some kind of sinful pervert because you're gender-variant. We are not on this earth to live a shame-filled lie that conveniently preserves and protects someone else's warped, pseudoreligious fantasy of how they think the world and everyone in it ought to be. We were created to live in the truth and the light of our uniquely transgender selves, to bless the world through our relational presence and our gifts, and to be in relationship with the God who created us in such wonderful human diversity.

God loves you with a deep, everlasting, unfathomable, incomprehensible love that will never, ever let you go. God loves you *because* you're transgender, not in spite of it; God loves you just because you're *you*. You are exactly as God created you. Your gender-variant mind, spirit, and body are worth more to God than all the gold, silver, and diamonds in the universe combined. Take pride (not vanity or arrogance, but quiet satisfaction and great joy) in the knowledge that you are loved, accepted, wanted, welcomed, and desired by your creator. Let that knowledge motivate you to take significant action on behalf of yourself and others who are oppressed in this world. "The promises of God are sure, and so too ought to be the status of those to whom the promises are made."[21] Saying *no* to shame; *no* to oppression; *no* to being marginalized; *no* to secrecy and silence; *no* to closets; *no* to a slow, agonizing spiritual and emotional (and sometimes physical) death by the denial of our transgender humanity; and *no* to second-class citizenship in the body of Christ is to shout a resounding *YES* to the God who gives us life and expects us to live it fully and passionately.

One of our major stumbling blocks to wholeness can be a simple lack of self-acceptance. Fear of ourselves can be a paralyzing factor, holding us back and keeping us from reaching our full human potential as God's beloved gender-variant persons. Ponder this amazing statement:

> Our deepest fear is not that we are inadequate. Our deepest fear is that we are powerful beyond measure. It is our light, not our darkness, that most frightens us. We ask ourselves, "Who am I to be brilliant, gorgeous, talented and fabulous?" Actually, who are you not to be? You are a child of God. Your playing small does not serve the world. There's nothing enlightened about shrinking so that other people won't feel insecure around you. We were born to make manifest the glory of God that is within us. It is not in just some of us, it is in everyone. And as we let our light shine, we unconsciously give other people permission to do the same. As we are liberated from our fears, our presence automatically liberates others.[22]

Although these challenging words have been widely credited to Nelson Mandela, actually he was quoting Marianne Williamson when he uttered them in his South African presidential inauguration speech. To know that Mandela lent his enormous moral credibility to Williamson's brilliant challenge is encouraging.

Nevertheless, accepting our greatness as manifestations of God's glory is not always an easy thing to ask of ourselves. We respect anyone who makes the courageous decision to live life on his or her own terms rather than on the terms of others. As we've already discovered, bravery isn't the absence of fear: bravery occurs when you're afraid but face your fear and do what must be done anyway. Betty Berzon comments,

> It takes courage to consult one's self for the direction to take in life rather than consulting tradition. It is often easier to be defined by what other people expect of you, to merge into a stereotype, to yield individuality, to abdicate responsibility for being who you are and becoming what you want to be. But the price for giving up the prerogative to grow is devastating in spirit, in energy, and in integrity. Forever, it seems, ["different"] people have been giving their power away to others: define me, explain me, structure my behavior, decide for me what I can and cannot hope to achieve in my life, make rules for my participation in society, let me know the limits of tolerability if I happen to go beyond the boundaries set for me.[23]

Berzon reiterates, "It takes uncommon courage to reclaim power once it has been given away. It is uncommon courage that is called for in developing a positive [transgender] identity in an anti [transgender] society."[24]

A story about Gandhi shows us the way:

> When summoned to London in 1931 to participate in a round-table discussion about responsible government (dominion status) for India, the great Indian statesman Mohandas Gandhi confronted the British Empire as a second-class citizen. He had no legal standing, was not a member of a political party, and spoke as an individual. Told by the British government that dominion status would eventually be given to India, Gandhi

looked the power structure squarely in the eye and informed the monocles that they needed to get out of India immediately. He did not speak about how long it would take. Gandhi simply remonstrated, "Quit India now!"[25]

Although the stage may be smaller, it takes no less courage for individual transgenderists to stand up for themselves and their community. As emancipated cross-dresser Lacey Leigh writes, "Growing numbers of us refuse to be anyone's doormat, punching bag, or social pariah any longer."[26] And Michael "Miqqui Alicia" Gilbert says, "The transgender community, cross-dressers, transgenderists, transsexuals and the entire panoply of gender diversity are not going away. We are here to stay. We are not harmful, not perverted, perhaps insidious, but absolutely and forever here."[27] Each of us gender-variant Christians must find our own ways to convey an equally firm and unequivocal message to the institutional church: "Stop patronizing us. Stop treating us as second-class citizens. We are free, we are equal, we are transgender, we are proud, and we demand our rights as Christians and as full members of the body of Christ. We won't stop to consider how long all this might take — that's not even open for discussion. Get over your fear and bigotry. In the name of Jesus, we demand our rights *now!*"

Our struggle for self-esteem as transgender Christians is not easy, particularly in light of the legalistic expectations of traditionalists within the church. But we must remember that our self-worth is not dependent upon the whims of a legalistic religion — it depends upon the fact that we are lovingly fashioned in the very image of God. Truluck says, "Legalism is an idolatrous religion. Idolatry is the result of making anything other than God absolute. When laws and rules become absolute, the individual is absorbed into the system and loses identity and self-esteem. Legalistic religion is the mortal enemy of healthy self-esteem."[28]

In the end, it's all about self-actualization through liberating our spirits, our pride as human beings, our minds and self-understanding, our relationships with God and with others, our potential to become all that we're capable of being. The reason for pursuing that liberation is always transformation — transformation into something more, something better than we are or have ever been. As womanist theologian Emilie M. Townes has written, "Liberation is the process of struggling with ourselves and with each other that begets the transformation of all of us to our full humanity."[29]

According to Scripture, Jesus too was frightened as he prayed in Gethsemane for deliverance from his impending suffering and death. But, like Jesus, we must confront our fears and make the bold, sacred choice to do God's work anyway. We must find our courage, find our truth, find our voice, find new ways to live our gender-variant, fully human lives openly and without apology for all to witness. Only then may we live into a full frontal faith that edifies and blesses our world. May God strengthen our hearts, minds, and spirits for that most worthy and beneficial of endeavors.

Chapter 9

WILDERNESS PILGRIMS AND PROPHETS

☿ JUST AS DELORES S. WILLIAMS makes the Genesis story of Hagar (Gen. 16:1–16; 21:1–21) a paradigm for understanding black women's struggles,[1] Hagar's story can also be a way of understanding the status of transgender people in the contemporary church. Through no fault of her own Hagar and her son were sent out into the wilderness to fend for themselves; in that apparently barren environment Hagar encountered God and received the promise that not only would she and Ishmael survive, but their seed would be multiplied and would become "a great nation." Ordinarily in the Bible such promises were delivered only to patriarchs, so Hagar "steps into the usual male role" by receiving that promise. By naming the one who had spoken to her *El Roi,* and hence naming the well at which the encounter occurred, "Hagar's authority substitutes for male authority," because the naming of shrines and sacred wells was usually reserved for men. Furthermore, Hagar turns out to be "the only person in the Bible to whom is attributed the power of naming God."[2] Despite being rejected by Sarah and Abraham, "with the aid of God, Ishmael and Hagar maintained an autonomous existence." Eventually Hagar again assumed the male role by finding an Egyptian wife for her son, thus founding her own "house" or tribe, and perpetuating in her "house" the Egyptian custom that inheritance passes through the mother, not the father.[3]

We suggest Hagar as a transgender paradigm not only because transgender oppression stems from the same mind-set that oppresses black women, and not only because of all the female-to-male gender-role shifts that occur during her story, but because like Hagar, we who are gender-variant discover ourselves to be wanderers in the wilderness of Christian nonacceptance. Many of us are gender-variant pilgrims in search of a spiritual home that we can call our own, a place where we can live and contribute as equals and as valued members in the family of God. Our wilderness journey is often difficult, and the road can be long, treacherous, and barren. Yet, despite these obstacles, there is a life-giving well and a wonderful promise at the end of this arduous path of faith: the promise of God to love us, to bless our lives, and to accept us unconditionally as beloved members of the Christian family. That promise explains why so many of us continue on the journey, for without the hope and promise of God's inclusive welcome we would have surely given up long ago.

"Promise" is a wonderful word. Webster defines it as a "basis for expectation." People need to hear and experience the inspiring, life-affirming promises and the divine expectations that God offers. Gender-variant persons are in a unique position to proclaim and live out those promises daily. Our gender-based outsider/outlaw status somehow enables us to envision and experience God's grace intimately even as we struggle with the vagaries of our existence here on this earth.

PROPHETIC TRANSGENDERISM

It's no accident that the roles of prophet and visionary have often been assumed by transgender persons throughout the centuries. Frequently, however, and much like Jesus himself, we gender-variant folk have been prophets without honor in our own country.[4] For Christians, who regard the Bible as divinely inspired, Epimenides forms a perfect example of a transgender prophet honored by God but without honor among most Christians. As Virginia mentioned in chapter 3, Epimenides was a poet from Crete who lived six centuries before Christ, who wore a mixture of masculine and feminine sacred attire and has been compared to the transsexual prophet Tiresias. In the New Testament, the apostle Paul quotes his words, calling him a "prophet" whose "witness is true" (Titus 1:12–13). In the famous sermon preached on Mars Hill in Athens, Paul again quotes Epimenides in a favorable context (Acts 17:28).[5] One would think that so much honor accorded in the Bible to a transgender homoerotic male would have deeply affected Christian attitudes toward both gayness and transgenderism, but as we all know, that has not been the case. If the lack of honor toward this prophet is based on ignorance, then part of our work is to publicize such aspects of transgender history.

An important element of the mystery of transgenderism appears to be an increased ability, perhaps even a uniquely God-given aptitude, to see the world and its people in new and different ways. This is not necessarily true for every gender-variant person (because sweeping generalizations are inherently unfair), but it seems to be a somewhat common characteristic for many of us. Our distinctive transgender status and life experiences appear to make us extremely well suited to the positions of visionary or prophet. It's a strange paradox that we are, on the one hand, outsiders who are marginalized by the church while, alternatively, many of us possess the God-given ability to view the world and the human condition with unique clarity from a remarkably different perspective, an ethos that offers a great deal of insight and wisdom for those who are willing to pay attention. The unfolding future, the shifting of paradigms, and the advancement of thought and behavior can always be more clearly observed and comprehended from the margins rather than from the center. It's much easier to see the horizon when you're already living out on the frontier.

Gender-variant people thus have a critical role to play in society: despite our enforced marginalized status we are the harbingers, the representatives, the embodiment, and often the actual agents of cultural change. Who better to personify change than those whose gender-variant identities and orientations are themselves symbolic of God's delight in human diversity? Ironically enough, change is simultaneously the best and the worst of what life has to offer. It's the worst because change always involves a death of some kind: the death of an old idea, the death of a previous way of thinking about or doing something, the death of a former way of life, the death of a paradigm or a tradition. Change is also the best part of life because change allows us to progress and move into the future, into a fullness of life, into the transforming richness of whatever it is that God has in store for us as individuals and as a community of faith.

Some people recoil from gender-variant persons because we seem to represent the death of their old, comfortable, tradition-steeped socioreligious ideal. In us they see the potential loss of all that brings them security, and they find that idea deeply threatening to their peace of mind. That's certainly understandable, but we would argue that by remaining frozen in their old paradigm they miss out on the myriad possibilities that a new, more enlightened frame of reference regarding gender can bring. They forego the delights and unique growth experiences that could come from welcoming transgender people into their lives. They forego the opportunity to experience the accepting, welcoming love of God for themselves and others. Subconsciously, those who resist change tend to exist in an unnamed yet constant state of mourning for a new, more meaningful, as-yet-unimagined life, a life that might be. Let us resolve to move past our self-imposed grief and fear into the joys and new possibilities that inevitably appear when we embrace each other as fully human and infinitely valuable solely because we are God's beloved people.

STRUGGLING TO BE WHOLE

As Kathleen D. Billman writes: "As a Christian I understand the struggle for wholeness for all people as God's saving work in the world, in which we are called to participate. Our hope is rooted in God's activity in our midst, but our eyes are also open to the depths of human tragedy and the cries of absence that are often deeply part of the Christian life."[6]

What the church has so far failed to realize or admit is that it *needs* transgenderists as part of God's saving work in the world. Christianity needs our strength of character; our spiritual gifts; our passion, wisdom, and insight; our experiences, knowledge, and perspectives; and most of all, our physical and spiritual presence. That's why, as God's much-loved gender-variant people, our responsibility is to become increasingly open and visible whenever and wherever we can, thereby demonstrating vividly that we are already here inside the church and that Christianity is, in fact, incomplete without us. Our lives and witness can help show the church and the world what is possible for human beings.

However, we transgender Christians are also missing out on something: In the end, we cannot be spiritually whole people unless we find ways to be part of the larger community of faith. We need the church just as much as it needs us. It's a peculiarly symbiotic relationship; each party is essential to the other for true spiritual health, even though it's often difficult for either faction to grasp and then act beneficially or reciprocally upon that paradoxical reality. In a larger sense, all lives are interrelated. Each of us exists in an inescapable system of mutuality. Our human destinies are inextricably linked.

WHY WE NEED INCLUSIVE LANGUAGE

The institutional church and its individual members must honestly consider and respond to the following question: Do we represent the love of Christ to those who are different, or are we merely demanding their conformity to our arbitrary norms in terms of dress and behavior so we can feel more comfortable and save ourselves potential dis-ease or awkwardness?

An important element of the needed transformation in the church involves the acceptance and use of inclusive language. Why is that important? Because the way we speak affects the way we think; the way we think affects the way we act; and the way we act affects the way we speak. It's worth remembering that at one time Sen. Trent Lott (R-Mississippi), as Senate majority leader, was one of the most powerful men in the world. Now he is not, all because of something he said. Behold the power of language.

We're aware that some people dismiss the idea of inclusive language as a frivolous or perhaps even dangerous exercise, one that supposedly attempts to create a "feminine" God to appease "militant feminists" and other purported left-wing radicals who seemingly reject traditional, male-oriented religious verbiage and understandings. But in actuality, inclusive language is not an attempt to remake God at all; that is not and never has been the point. Instead, the language of spiritual inclusivity is an attempt to create a positive, affirming Christian environment that includes and reflects and speaks to the living realities of *all* people who are created in God's image, not just white, heterosexual males.

Far from "remaking God," inclusive language would *reclaim* the God of the Bible, who is depicted in a remarkable multitude of images that add up to a transgender and even transspecies oneness. It seems logical that the biblical authors, educated in an overwhelmingly patriarchal environment, would seek to pay reverence to the Deity by referring to "him" in terms that conveyed honor in their culture: husband, father, law-giver, creator, king, warrior, conqueror, and so forth. Therefore we must wonder: what, other than divine inspiration, caused those authors also to depict God as a midwife, a nursing mother, a beloved female, a homemaker, a mother bear, a female pelican, a mother eagle, or as Dame Wisdom, not to mention God as rock, wind, water, fire, oil, and the androgynous dove?[7] Widespread Christian failure to honor the diversity of biblical imagery in its language is no accident; it is an attempt to keep power in the hands of those who already possess it.

The Reverend Dr. Christie Cozad Neuger writes, "There has long been the clear understanding that language not only reflects reality but also creates it. When the language of the culture [in this case, the Christian culture] does not carry the experience or perspective of women or others of nondominant cultural status, then the culture will not operate in the best interests of those groups. And not only are the people in these groups deprived of empowerment and full participation in the culture, but the culture is damaged, too."[8] Therefore, inclusive language is an attempt to incorporate the experiences and perspectives of nondominant persons (or nonwhites, nonheterosexuals, nonmales), thus empowering them and permitting their full participation in the central life of the culture. Additionally, the widespread use of inclusive language would keep the Christian culture itself from becoming even more damaged than it already is by helping to reverse the trend of negativity toward "difference" that has been prevalent for so long.

DESTRUCTIVE ADAPTATION

In *A Feminist Position on Mental Health,* authors Mary Ballou and Nancy Gabalac discuss the systemic disempowerment, the loss of personal and communal voice, and the harmful adaptation that occurs among nondominant groups in our society. The authors describe a skewed yet socially approved and practically ubiquitous developmental process. This systematic pedagogy teaches minority groups and individuals to adapt, in a perilous and often highly damaging manner, to the dominant culture's arbitrary definitions regarding acceptability.

Ballou and Gabalac have outlined a five-stage process for this destructively adaptive thought and behavior method of social control: humiliation (reduction of one's self in one's own eyes and in the eyes of others), inculcation (discovering the social rules and expectations), retribution (punishment for breaking the rules), conversion (coming to believe or buy into the dominant culture's limiting and oppressive ideas), and conscription (persuading others of the "correctness" of the dominant culture's definitions and rules).[9]

This debilitating adaptive process accurately describes what happens to most transgender persons in our society and its institutions. The process of harmful adaptation begins in our youth and is continued throughout adulthood. Gender-variant people are humiliated and reduced because of what we are; we quickly learn the rules for acceptable dress and behavior; when we don't conform to those rules we are punished; many of us are eventually converted into believing the culture's lies about the "inherent dichotomous nature" of gender; and many go on to actively promote that insidious binary gender paradigm to others.

The damaging adaptive process creates, sustains, and encourages the lie of rigid, inflexible gender dichotomy based solely upon a partial understanding of anatomy, genitalia, DNA, and chromosomes, thereby creating a false social expectation that is unacceptable and unworkable for gender-variant individuals. We lose our beautiful, powerfully unique transgender voice through a socially enforced acceptance of the language of harmful adaptation. This loss of personal identity damages every part of the culture: gender-variant people, social relations in general, the church, families, business, educational organizations — every person and every institution. That's why everyone should learn about the systemic, limiting, abusive, gender-based lies that have been taught to us about who we are and who we can be.

Neuger explains, "Making choices against a system, even a destructive one, that has been deeply internalized as truth and that is persistently presented in culture as part of the natural order, is a frightening thing."[10] Nevertheless, we must come to a transforming awareness of this destructive adaptive paradigm, and then we must take action for the sake of empowering ourselves and of changing the culture, an oppressive, gender-polarized, restrictive culture that has been and continues to be toxic and even lethal to many of our transgender sisters and brothers. We must find ways to do this *together* because "the seductive and coercive strategies of the dominant culture are too strong for any one person to resist."[11] We must combine and thus multiply our strengths and our resources. If we are ever to achieve the goals of justice, liberation, and social equality, we must depend upon our collective imaginations; our concerted, unified efforts; and our relationship with the God who lovingly created us as gender-variant.

EMBRACING THE FLAME

Won't it be a blessed day when inclusive, respectful love and acceptance overcome our old, coercive socioreligious myths of form and arbitrary structure? Won't God smile broadly when we silly human beings can finally learn to love each other's uniqueness, live in mutual, reciprocal relationships, and be open to the eternal dance of change that leads to transformation? We don't have to discard tradition completely, but we surely must find new ways to develop living, growing traditions that move beyond the soul-killing stagnation of our old paradigms. These new traditions must become doorways to positive transformation through our interactions with God and with each other. We need transformation if we are to grow and become all we were meant to be, even though we seem to resist change and struggle against it with all our might. We may as well be prepared; when transformation is welcomed, lives and relationships and contexts will alter accordingly.

If we are to be the whole, healthy, relational people of God, we cannot continue living "inside the theological straitjackets that Christianity seems so eager to force upon people in every generation."[12] For gender-variant Christians, the issue is not so much the reality of God's presence in our lives; many of us already sense that and cannot be robbed of it. The issue is that we are continually reminded — by Christians, no less — that God and the body of Christ are, for all practical purposes, unavailable to us because of what we are.

This claim is particularly ironic, because the New Testament actually depicts Christ's body (the church) in a series of transgender images: the female church is instructed to grow up into the male head (Eph. 4:15); all Christians, including women and girls, are called Christ's brothers; all Christians, including men and boys, are called Christ's bride (Eph. 23–30); and all Christians are instructed to take off our egocentric concerns and cross-dress by "putting on the Sovereign Jesus Christ" like a garment (Rom. 13:14).[13] Despite all of that, we transgenderists have been pushed to the margins of our faith communities by an institutional Christian church that doesn't want or accept us. Yet, astoundingly enough, many of us still seek to enter and serve within the central, mainstream life of the church. That means transformation is in order, for the present operative system simply doesn't work for us (and it doesn't work for the institution of Christianity either, although the church is loathe to admit it).

Part of this transformative process must inevitably involve a willingness to accept the benign differences we find in each other, and to embrace those differences as holy manifestations of a loving and merciful God. In the end, it comes down to a conscious recognition and acknowledgment of the divinely given flame, the light that burns in each human being created in God's image. When we can learn to recognize and respect the authenticity of that gift of light, we will surely begin to treat each other with Christlike love as we work together to create justice and make peace on the earth.

Chapter 10

STEPS THAT LIE AHEAD

LILLA WATSON, Australian Aboriginal educator and activist, has said, "If you have come here to help me, you are wasting your time. . . . But if you have come because your liberation is bound up with mine, then let us work together."[1] We who care about justice and the integrity of the Christian church must consciously determine to take risks so we can move forward together in our struggle for personal, religious, and social freedom. Our liberation is indeed bound up with that of everyone else, and an unrisking life can never become an expanding life. Lilla Watson's understanding of our universal need for liberation ought to become a motivating force for any thinking person who cares about the souls of human beings.

Toward that end, all Christians have a responsibility and an obligation to address the specific needs of transgender persons within the church. We must take some calculated risks, risks that may perhaps make us grow uncomfortable or push us into unfamiliar territory. That's how life works. If we don't take some chances and become risk-takers, we don't grow. Instead, we stagnate. We cannot afford to give up or permit a lack of comfort or a state of unfamiliarity to keep us from doing the work of creating God's justice.

However, to do this work with effectiveness we must first become aware of four distinct yet interrelated concepts:

1. God loves each one of us unconditionally and has created all of humankind and the natural world to live together on this planet in astonishing diversity. Part of that divinely created (and therefore blessed and good) diversity includes and has always included the presence and gifts of gender-variant people.

157

2. Our culture and its institutions have created specific, arbitrary expectations for human beings, built around a damaging social construct of binary gender that amounts to male-female polarization. The embodied presence of gender-variant individuals is therefore of concern to society in many areas and for many reasons. The best (and, as far we can see, the only) way to alleviate that specific social concern is for transgender people to live lives of truth, integrity, honesty, and openness so that all may know the benign nature of our existence as well as the unique abilities and contributions we have to offer the world.

3. The church has a legitimate need for education and information about the realities of transgender life. This means we need to move far away from the tabloid sensationalism that is so predominant in the mass media. Sensationalism places the responsibility (as well as the marvelous opportunity) for educating the church squarely on the shoulders of gender-variant people, and not necessarily on those of academicians or mental health professionals.[2] Therefore, we must do all we can to tell our stories — to educate and inform others about the true nature of our gender gifts, about the realities of our gender-variant lives, and about the destructive consequences of oppressing and marginalizing anyone who wishes to be a contributing member of society and of the family of God.

4. Finally, life in this world is often paradoxical rather than completely rational or objective, particularly when it comes to matters of faith. The church must learn to greet paradox and ambiguity with joyful anticipation, not dread. "One plus one does not always equal two, and ministry needs to occur in a world where life is more gray than black and white."[3] If the church is serious about being an effective agent of Christ's ministry on earth, it must set aside its ancient fears and misgivings about the validity of transgender lives so it can begin doing the work of ministering to those who fall into the "gray" areas. Faithfulness to God's ministerial call demands no less.

TRANSCENDING CULTURAL CONDITIONING

Those "gray" areas are what create anxiety and confusion around issues of gender variance. As Terri Main puts it:

> For most people gender is one of the few certainties of life. It's something they think little about. They might be confused about their career choices, who they are going to marry, or their place in God's plan for this universe, but gender to them is a given. They can't even begin to understand how [transgenderists] feel, and so they often put it into the context of something they can understand....[4]

Main continues,

> Since they cannot understand our experience, they also cannot understand the pain we feel when they are accusing us ("warning" from their perspective) of sexual immorality or violating God's law when we know that we are living morally, and trying to do His [*sic*] will in our lives. They can't see the turmoil and pain inside of us when people we know and love are telling us that we are going to hell for a condition none of us asked for and can't do anything about.[5]

All of us who claim to be Christian need to forget about forcing everyone into easily manageable black and white boxes, and we must start seeing people as the complex, uniquely created and gifted entities they were created to be. We church members must begin asking ourselves, "What can we, as the compassionate, loving people of God, do to include everyone without judgment and punishment?"

This problem reaches far beyond the transgender community. Judgmentalism, religious bigotry, and injustice are practiced daily against people of many different minority groups, and we would all be better off if we could learn to dispense with our arbitrary, unfounded judgments of others who may be different in some way. We must become a people of faith who are open to receiving new possibilities for understanding, growth, and acceptance of the inevitable and delightful differences that exist within the human condition.

In this culture, gender training starts practically at birth, and such training is extremely pervasive. Many studies demonstrate that gender instruction begins in early infancy[6] and that adults interact differently with, and even see different qualities in, an infant when that *same infant* is designated as either a boy or a girl. "Explicit instances of selective gender socialization are only the tip of the iceberg";[7] any Christian who cares about justice-love must campaign for egalitarian child rearing that honors children's gender as God-given and desirable rather than attempting to mold them into what society thinks they ought to be. In short, we must learn to "receive the children," as Jesus did.

VALUING OUR OWN TRANSGENDER TRAITS WITHOUT OVERVALUING THEM

To value our own transgender traits properly means neither to undervalue them nor to overvalue them. Most of this book emphasizes the importance of transcending our culturally induced tendency to undervalue our gender-variant qualities; now a few words are in order to help us achieve a healthful balance.

Like undervaluing, overvaluing is a symptom of low self-esteem. In its fear and alienation, each human ego imagines itself separate from God and Her other creatures, seizing upon diversity as a means of setting up hierarchies in which some of us are more entitled to the good basics of life (including respect!) than others are. Whether we overvalue or undervalue our particular traits and experiences doesn't really matter to our separated egos because either way, we are using our differences to judge others and push them away.

For instance, as a lesbian Virginia has met heterosexists who consider themselves superior to her because they are sure that heterosexuality is God's will for everyone. She has also met certain heterosexuals who feel guilty about their more privileged social status and seem to wish they shared her oppression so that they could feel better about themselves. She calls this emotion "liberal guilt," and she has felt it herself concerning her white, middle-class American privilege. Vanessa, too, has struggled with that same liberal guilt syndrome as it applies to her privileged biological (male), racial (white), and economic (American middle-class) status.

Unfortunately, liberal guilt throws up a wall of imagined inferiority just as surely as self-righteousness throws up a wall of imagined superiority. Better by far that each of us should learn to appreciate our own social location, rejoice for those who seem to have it better than we, seek to alleviate the sufferings of those who have less than we, and do whatever we can to bring about a more equitable distribution of resources in this world!

From the perspective of time, our particularities matter a great deal. Vanessa has expended enormous time and energy learning to value herself as a cross-dressing husband and father. Virginia has expended no less time and energy learning to value herself as a masculine lesbian partner, mother, and grandmother, and much additional time and energy coping with her disability (severe arthritis). No matter how you may identify, everyone who reads these words will have invested hugely in whatever particularities set your human experiences apart from those of many other people.

But from the standpoint of eternity, our bodily particularities are not much more than tiny blips on a tremendous radar screen. All of us come into this world "trailing clouds of glory/From God, who is our home."[8] All of us have to do the work of liberating ourselves from the shadows of the various prison-houses that close in upon us and limit our freedom in this world. All of us have to train our minds to focus on the sacred ground that undergirds forms and appearances, instead of focusing on the forms and appearances alone. And all of us need one another to help us accomplish our purpose of growing up into the fullness of the one who perfectly mirrors our source (Eph. 4:15). So our diversities are not *ultimately* important, even though penultimately, here in this world, they are very important. If we let them, they will make it possible for us to do the work of justice-love in ways that are uniquely our own. As each of us completes our unique section of the quilt, the whole body of Christ is knit together in ways far too splendid to require any illusions of less or more, superiority or inferiority. Ultimately, we are all one.

BEARING ONE ANOTHER'S BURDENS,
TRANSGENDERLY AND TENDERLY

An injunction familiar to most Christians is found in Galatians 6:12: "Bear one another's burdens, and in this way you will fulfill the law of Christ." We think this injunction carries a special intensity for those of us who are transgender. Just as it would be exploitation to engage in sex with a person for whom you felt no concern or no desire to contribute to that person's well-being and happiness, we think it short-circuits transgender Christianity to enjoy the benefits of partial or even total identification with the other sex/gender without bearing any of the burdens of that sex/gender.

For instance, it seems to us important for women who also identify as masculine to learn empathy with the plight of ordinary men in modern society. Such women already know the burdens of women and of being transgender; but it is Christlike for them also to try to alleviate the sufferings of their brothers. In her monumental study entitled *Stiffed: The Betrayal of the American Man* (New York: Wm. Morrow, 1999), Susan Faludi describes the disappointment felt by American males as they find themselves unable to meet the impossible requirements of modern masculinity — namely, that to be a "real man" is to be the master of one's universe, always in control of everything and everyone. As a matter of fact, manliness has been construed in different ways by different societies: in Japan, manliness is diligence and discipline; in Cyprus, it is focused on male companionship outside the home; in Mexico, it is supporting a family; and so forth. Therefore, manliness is a cultural construct, just like womanliness: a symbolic script contingent on the culture and the era.[9] The script handed to contemporary American men is a recipe for failure and for the violent resentment and frustration that failure can fuel. Vanessa knows something about that All-American manliness script; she has struggled her entire life to develop and maintain an equanimity between those masculine cultural expectations and her own innate feminine characteristics that cry out for transgender expression.

Men are told to take responsibility for being the dominant sex, but a great many of them feel utterly dominated and even crushed by corporate structures, industrial downsizing, betrayal by the owners of sports teams, idiotic portrayals in the media, their perception of women's power, and the like. Faludi covers 608 pages with carefully documented evidence that most men do not feel the reins of power in their hands, but rather feel power's bit in their mouths. So they cling to a phantom status. The level of cultural mockery and animosity directed at men who step out of line is enough to force many men to try desperately to preserve the pretense that they are fully in control, even when they know better in their hearts.

The cure for this crisis of modern manhood lies in learning to be fully human, no longer living by a "masculinity scorecard" but working together with women to create a more just, free, human world. Transgenderists, with our mixture of masculinity and femininity, are in a perfect position to help provide models for this inner transformation that will in turn transform society. In particular, Christian women who are lesbian, or masculine, or career-oriented, or drag kings, can refuse merely to skim off sensations of powerfulness from the social construct of manliness, instead listening to the pain of ordinary men and through nonjudgmental respect helping them find their way toward a more profoundly centered humanhood.

Conversely, male cross-dressers can help to bear the burdens of women by refusing to stop at the wigs, high heels, cosmetics, and coffee klatches (fine as they may be), by moving also toward a genuine sharing of what it means to be a woman in this world. For instance, married cross-dressers can share in the work it takes to run a household — the cooking, the cleaning, the childcare — as a profound way of expressing their feminine component. Outside the home, men can cooperate with women's organizations to achieve justice for women in the church, the workplace, politics, medicine, law, and everywhere else that egalitarianism and fairness have long been denied.

It seems hardly fair to skim off the pleasures of femininity without also picking up the less attractive aspects of what the binary gender construct assigns as women's social roles. By refusing to support traditional gender roles — "men's work" versus "women's work" — transgender men can empower the women in their lives to view themselves as fully human, worthy of respect, and equal partners in the construction of a healthier society.

Transsexuals, having lived as both male and female, are in a remarkable position to help all the rest of us grasp what manhood and womanhood entail in a sex/gender polarized society like our own. For instance, when she had completed her transition from male to female, Kate Bornstein was given a job that carried greater responsibility than her former work and paid significantly less — pointing up the sex/gender financial inequity that cries to heaven to be redressed. (Women do the vast majority of the world's work, but own precious little of the world's wealth.) In 1997 in the United States, 55 percent of single mothers and 61 percent of displaced homemakers were living at or below the poverty line, and the situation has worsened since then.[10]

For another instance, Rev. Erin Swenson (formerly Eric) noticed after her transition from male to female that for some reason she was frequently colliding with men. Finally she figured out what was wrong: seeing a woman approaching, men kept on walking straight ahead on their course, unconsciously assuming she would get out of the way; but she, having grown up as a male, did not realize that as a woman she would be expected to step aside. Who knew that this sort of dominance and submission was occurring? It takes transgender insight to alert us to such unconsciously hierarchical behaviors.

Vanessa has learned firsthand that women must always be concerned with their own personal safety whenever they're out in public. When she's dressed as a man, she usually never has to worry or think much at all about where she's going, what the circumstances are, what people might be around her, whether there are any potential dangers or threats to her person, or what the overall safety factor might be. These concerns don't usually enter into the equation for most men; usually they just get up and go wherever they like without a care or a second thought. But when Vanessa is dressed as a woman, all those factors and more must be considered and continually evaluated on a moment-to-moment basis from the time she leaves her doorstep until she returns to the safety of her home. Vanessa has become significantly aware of the underlying fear of attack or rape that women must confront every day of their lives. Unfortunately, most American men don't truly comprehend the scope of the issue or that the women in their lives are constantly dealing with this critical concern.

Susan Faludi, who spent a lot of time interviewing men who were involved in the evangelical movement called Promise Keepers, points out that the men she hung out with did not seem very invigorated to construct their marriages along the lines of Ephesians 5:22, "Wives, submit to your husbands."[11] No wonder they weren't invigorated! In Greek, Ephesians 5:22 contains no verb of its own; instead, it leans upon the verb in the previous verse, because Ephesians 5:21 is the controlling statement for the passage to follow. It is addressed to all Christians without regard for sex/gender: "Be subject to one another out of reverence for Christ." The point of Ephesians 5:21–33 is mutual subjection, mutual supportiveness, mutual reverence. Mutuality invigorates marriages, partnerships, and general human relationships — not a one-way domination that stifles intimacy and love.

Just as we transgender people learn to honor all aspects of our nature without too much regard for what society insists must remain either masculine or feminine, the human race in general must learn to do equal honor to all of its members, which is especially true of those who claim membership in the body of Christ, the new humanity. We who are transgender have felt the sting of rejection, of being treated as second class, or worse. Let us take care never to pass that sting on to anyone else! Instead, let us reach across traditional sex/gender categories to fulfill Christ's law by bearing one another's burdens.

BUILDING A TRANSGENDER COMMUNITY

During the winter of 2001, an interreligious service was planned in a major city to honor the memory of transgender people who had been murdered for being who they were. Many organizations were involved, the date was set, and a major church sanctuary was secured. But at the last moment the whole event was canceled. Why? Because leaders in some organizations did not like the way leaders in other groups were handling certain organizational details. Everyone lost —

especially the transgender people of that city, who at that time could have used a good dose of hope, unity, and respect.

We can't think of anything that our detractors would enjoy more than the sight of transgender, lesbian, gay, and bisexual organizations squabbling among themselves and canceling important community events because of those squabbles. Detractors would also be pleased to know about certain lesbians who want nothing to do with male-to-female transsexuals ("womyn-born-womyn only!"), certain cross-dressers and transsexuals who are homophobic, certain gay males who scorn effeminate men, certain gays and lesbians who are contemptuous of bisexuals, and other lateral violence within the GLBT movement. So we want to offer some further musings about building genuine transgender Christian *community*.

First, and whether anyone likes it or not, the most visible trans-gender people in society are also the ones who are the most influential in terms of creating and defining community for the rest of us. By their presence and visibility alone, these persons are the ones who often critically determine what society thinks of gender-variant persons and how we are perceived on a cultural level. Transgenderist Pat Conover writes that "it is transgender people who are out and participating in transgender groups and activities, or are known as transgender people in the larger society, who most influence any emerging trans-gender community as well as influencing societal views of transgender people."[12] That's one reason that we must become more media-savvy as a community, for perception is the great arbiter in our culture and the mass media is the social shaper of perception. How we are viewed by the public is directly related to how we present ourselves, how people see us, how we behave and treat others, and how we are thus considered to be assets or detriments to society.

Our society's capitalistic economy encourages us to think in terms of self-interest, personal power, and looking out for number one. But Jesus depicted God's essence not as power, but as compassion, and he instructed his followers to become as compassionate as their Source. The conventional concerns of Jesus' day were family, wealth, personal honor, and religion, but Jesus' radical teaching was that all of these worthy concerns were *rivals* to what ought to be our deepest concern: centering ourselves in the love of God that includes everyone and everything. As Marcus Borg puts it, the challenge Jesus offers is "to see things as they really are — namely, [that] at the heart of everything is a reality that is in love with us."[13] In love with *all* of us! And if we don't love our transgender sisters and brothers whom we have seen, how can we love God, whom we have not seen (1 John 4:20–21)?

If Christian churches had fulfilled their prophetic calling of speaking the truth to power, Jesus' views about inclusive community would be common knowledge and practice in our culture. Instead, because so many churches have not taken a prophetic and liberative stance, society has become more and more individualistic, less and less concerned about the common good. In such a fractured, alienated society it is difficult to remember that we were created for community, and that our full maturity requires relatedness within community. We cannot know fully who we are until we see what we can do in relationship to others. Although our capitalist society values autonomy and self-reliance as the fullest realization of personhood, in actuality an authentically human person is someone who acts in relation to others. The person's character is disclosed by the quality of his/her words and actions in the context of relationship, not of isolation and individualism. The way we treat others is the yardstick by which our character is measured.

Although our society rigidly views family as a closed-system nesting of one male, one female, and any children they may engender, Jesus views family as everyone who shares his values (Matt. 12:48–49). Furthermore, the Bible depicts the marital relationship in a very countercultural fashion, in terms of the corporate and universal body of Christ (Eph. 5:21–33). The implication of this imagery is that erotic love ideally becomes a means of embracing all existence everywhere, for it is "in [Christ that] all things hold together" (Col. 1:17). Love of one other person is intended to provide a foundation for universal communion.

In this connection, Roman Catholic theologian Catherine Mowry LaCugna emphasizes that God is "self-communicating, existing from all eternity in relation to another [in a coequal and loving Trinity]."[14]

Therefore, "the ultimate ground and meaning of being is [not a self-sustaining solitary figure but] communication among persons. God is ecstatic, fecund, self-emptying out of love for another, a personal God who comes to self through another."[15] Being fearfully and wonderfully made in the image of that personal, loving, trinitarian God, we too come to self through others. That makes our relationships sacred, and they deserve to be treated as such.

Hebrew Bible scholar Walter Brueggemann clarifies our task as Christians in community: it is nothing less than reconciliation (2 Cor. 5:17–18). Reconciliation includes acts of solidarity with all the "little ones." Certainly transgender youth would be included among those "little ones," but also anyone who for any reason is relatively weak, poor, and/or disempowered. Most of our churches would rather practice charity *toward* the little ones than stand in solidarity *with* them, and Brueggemann explains why: Charity doesn't disturb existing power structures, and solidarity does. The giving of charity means maintaining one's position of power over another, while solidarity means choosing to give up and/or share power, to become equals, to rejoice in the empowerment of another. To the degree that churches and governments refuse to redistribute power by sharing it with the little ones, our job as Christians is to speak truth to them. And to the degree that we possess power — and all of us possess *some* power — to that degree "our ministry is . . . the empowerment of other [people] who until now have been denied power."[16]

BRINGING A DRAG QUEEN TO CHURCH

On June 16, 2002, the Reverend Canon Jay D. Wegman preached a sermon at New York's Cathedral of St. John the Divine. It was entitled "Bring a Drag Queen to Church." Canon Wegman was concerned that on July 7, 2002, the sexist, homophobic, and transphobic Anglican archbishop of Nigeria was to be honored at the cathedral (not for his bigotry, but for his work on behalf of economic justice and as a gesture of church unity). Wegman explained that the purpose of the Nigerian archbishop's visit to the United States was to call the Episcopal Church back toward "righteousness." In response, Canon

Wegman suggested that the archbishop be greeted by "a cathedral full of righteous transvestites." Wegman added that "the archbishop seems to have conveniently forgotten that Anglicanism was founded by a murderous adulterer [Henry VIII], that a woman guided its ethos and worship for its initial forty-five years [Elizabeth I], and that its primary text [the Bible] was translated under the close guidance of a celebrated bisexual [James I, namesake of the King James Bible, who was married and also had a bevy of boyfriends]."

If you don't happen to know a drag queen, Canon Wegman suggested, "bring your own inner drag queen. For somewhere deep within each and every one of us there is a fabulous person desperate to break free from the restraints imposed by others and be the person you truly are."[17] Now, this sounds like real Christianity — a church willing to minister to everyone beloved by the heart of God, including the badly mistaken archbishop as well as the righteous transvestites and all the closeted drag kings and queens and other identities of all the world!

Wegman's invitation sounds in fact like an authentic witness to the way of Jesus. Remember that for centuries Jesus was depicted by artists as gender-variant, long before the concept or word "transgender" was developed. Early Christian artists usually portrayed Jesus as having a decidedly feminine comportment; various poets expressed their devotion to Jesus in homoerotic terms, Thomas Traherne calling himself Christ's Ganymede[18] and John Donne calling himself Christ's bride. Roman Catholic priests have for centuries been encouraged to see Christ as their bridegroom. Meanwhile, traditional public discourse has stripped Jesus of all libido, making him into an asexual eunuch. But the Santerias of Buenos Aires openly venerate Santa Librada, the crucified WomanChrist, a divine gender-blending of Mary and Jesus. Knowing that cross-dressing and role-reversal are socially taboo, Jesus acts like a transsexual when he kneels like a slave girl to wash the feet of his disciples or makes a hero out of the religiously outcast Samaritan. Since Jesus apparently was neither married nor celibate,[19] he was certainly one of the sexual minorities of his place and time; and if he is understood as having literally been born of a virgin, he must also be regarded as phenotypically male and chromosomally female (that is, as intersexual).[20] Vanessa devoted an entire chapter of *Crossing Over* to a discussion of the church's struggle with its own transgender identity. That chapter included an examination of a transgender Christ, that is, Jesus as metaphorical cross-dresser, a startlingly unique idea offered by Vicar Eleanor McLaughlin.[21] So for Canon Wegman to invite drag queens and other transgenderists to church is not unseemly at all, but certainly a far more Christian witness than excluding or marginalizing us could ever be.

As they stood together amid the ruin and desolation of his war-torn village in Guatemala, an unnamed man once told the Reverend Rebecca Voelkel, "You can't do the work of justice and resurrection without a dream and a vision of what you are working for. And you can't survive over the long haul if you don't bring the dream and vision of God's great celebration and banquet to the here and now. Only claiming the joy right now enables you to go on each day. . . . If I can't dance, I won't be part of your revolution."[22] Claiming our own dream, our own vision, and our own joy while becoming partners in the dance of God's relational love now becomes both our task and our opportunity as we confront injustice and work to create peace in our world.

In a society like ours, many find it easier to take off all their physical clothes than to express the human vulnerability and compassion that Jesus asks of us in what we have called full frontal faith. The Big Question of our lives is this: Are we willing to "grow up in every way into [the One] who is the head, into Christ" (Eph. 4:15)? That would entail not only accepting our inner drag people but also cooperating with others in a massive transgender challenge to the church, a challenge to become everything it was meant to be as the all-inclusive body of Christ. Growing up would entail bearing one another's burdens, struggling with difficult issues together, yet viewing ourselves and others as equally beautiful and beloved in a universal sibling-hood. In short to take a transgender journey toward a full frontal faith, and nothing less, is our high calling in Christ Jesus.

The response is up to us.

NOTES

Introduction: Welcome to This Exploration!

1. In this book we have chosen to use the word *transgender*, not transgende*red*, for the same reasons offered by John Shelby Spong in his book *A New Christianity for a New World: Why Traditional Faith Is Dying and How a New Faith Is Being Born* (San Francisco: HarperSanFrancisco, 2001). In his endnotes Spong writes that *transgendered* "implies something that has been done to a person. We never say that one has been *maled* or *femaled*; we should likewise call no one *transgendered*" (255). We agree with this reasoning. This is a new linguistic understanding and an important, gender-based nuance that we recommend to all people when discussing gender-variant individuals.

2. Not that we consider transgender issues more important than many other justice issues. Ending world hunger, distributing wealth more equitably, providing health care for those who cannot afford it, counteracting the oppression of nonwhite people and of women and children worldwide — all these and more are certainly matters of life-and-death importance. But our calling right now is to write this book as our contribution to correcting one aspect of an interlocked web of injustice. If everyone listens carefully for his/her authentic calling and makes active response to it, the entire web of systemic injustice will eventually be corrected. But when injustices are as intricately involved in one another as they are, it is counterproductive to assume that because we ourselves are called to address one certain injustice, our calling makes that injustice more basic and important than any other. Not so, as we have learned from friends who are black, female, poor, disabled, and transgender. Which of the multiple oppressions is more basic, more important? None. They are interwoven and mutually reinforcing. To struggle against one is to struggle against all. No one person can work on every front simultaneously. But each of us can do what we are called to do in the awareness that each injustice interacts with every other, so that making a "hierarchy of oppressions" is inaccurate and unwise. In this spirit we write, passionately yet painstakingly, about transgender liberation.

Chapter 1: Equipping for the Journey

1. Tucker Lieberman, *www.angelfire.com/ri/tucker/gender/gender.html.*

2. Ibid.

3. Michael "Miqqui Alicia" Gilbert, *The Transgendered Philosopher,* online at *www.symposion.com/ijt/gilbert/gilbert.htm.*

4. Julie Ann Johnson, "Foreword," in *By the Grace of God,* ed. Julie Ann Johnson (Wheaton, Ill.: SSP Publications, 2001), 17.

5. Becky Allison, "Work It Out," in *By the Grace of God,* 260.

6. Kim Ode, "In This World, Rev. Graham, No Two Ways about It," *Minneapolis Star Tribune,* August 14, 2002, E2.

7. Pat Conover, *Transgender Good News* (Silver Spring, Md.: New Wineskin Press, 2002), 68.

8. Ibid., 72–73.

9. See md_2003's *Amazon.com* customer review for Jason Cromwell, *Transmen and FTMs: Identities, Bodies, Genders, and Sexualities* (Urbana: University of Illinois Press, 1999).

10. Gilbert, *The Transgendered Philosopher.*

11. Gianna E. Israel, *A Parent's Dilemma: The Transgender Child,* online at *www.firelily.com/gender/gianna/dilemma.html.*

12. Paul Cody, *Suicide and Gay, Lesbian, Bisexual and Transgender Youth,* from *www.unhcc.unh.edu/glbtsuicide.html.*

13. Ibid.

14. Christine M. Smith, *Risking the Terror: Resurrection in This Life* (Cleveland: Pilgrim Press, 2001), 13.

15. As a beginning, we recommend perusing the Synchronicity Bookstore of the International Foundation for Gender Education, online at *www.ifge.org.* This organization has a variety of books available on many transgender subjects. As a general rule any book more than ten years old is probably outdated and may contain incomplete or inaccurate information on transgender issues. Research into gender variance has increased in the last decade or so, and new data continue to appear as further studies are mounted. However, much more investigation is needed into the many unanswered questions about the origins and varied manifestations of transgender orientations and behaviors. Our hope is that such critical information will become increasingly available as additional research is pursued and documented.

16. Viktor E. Frankl, *Man's Search for Meaning* (Boston: Beacon Press, 1992), 114–15.

17. Marcus J. Borg and N. T. Wright, *The Meaning of Jesus: Two Visions* (San Francisco: HarperSanFrancisco, 1989), 9.

18. Smith, *Risking the Terror,* 6.

19. Ibid., 9.

Chapter 2: Reordering Our Travel Priorities

1. John W. Gardner, "Self-Renewal," *Futurist* (November–December 1996).

2. Jack Trout and Steve Rivkin, *The New Positioning* (New York: McGraw-Hill, 1996), 21.

3. Surya Monro, "Transphobia," in *Gendy's Journal*, online at *www .gender.org.uk/gendys/journal/15surya.htm.*

4. Jack Rogers, *Confessions of a Conservative Evangelical*, 2d ed. (Louisville: Geneva Press, 2001), 11.

5. Ibid., 8, 132.

6. Christine M. Smith, *Risking the Terror: Resurrection in This Life* (Cleveland: Pilgrim Press, 2001), 43.

7. Kathleen D. Billman, "Pastoral Care As an Art of Community," in *The Arts of Ministry: Feminist-Womanist Approaches*, ed. Christie Cozad Neuger (Louisville: Westminster John Knox Press, 1996), 15.

8. Ibid.

9. As cited by Karen Armstrong, *The Battle for God* (New York: Ballantine Books, 2000), xiii.

10. Ibid., xviii.

11. Please don't be put off or angered by Armstrong's use of the word *myth* in conjunction with Christianity. Some people become instantly ready to take up arms and go to war whenever Bible stories are referred to as myths, but this is generally an overreaction. *Myth* is a perfectly appropriate word for Armstrong to use in this context. *The American Heritage Dictionary of the English Language*, 4th ed. (Boston: Houghton Mifflin, 2000) defines *myth* as "a traditional, typically ancient story dealing with supernatural beings [such as God], ancestors [like the patriarchs of the Pentateuch], or heroes [like Moses, David, Jesus, and so forth] that serves as a fundamental type in the worldview of a people, as by explaining aspects of the natural world or delineating the psychology, customs, or ideals of society: *the myth of Eros and Psyche; a creation myth.*" So we see that use of the word *myth* creates no legitimate reason for anyone to feel threatened — it's simply a cultural reference and an archetypal tool, not a subversive attempt to dismiss the validity of Christian beliefs.

12. Armstrong, *The Battle for God*, 355.

13. Ibid., 366.

14. Christine E. Gudorf, "The Erosion of Sexual Dimorphism: Challenges to Religion and Religious Ethics," *Journal of the American Academy of Religion* 69 (December 2001): 863–91.

15. Reverend Dr. William R. Johnson, "Protestantism and Gay and Lesbian Freedom," in *Positively Gay: New Approaches to Gay and Lesbian Life* (Berkeley, Calif.: Celestial Arts, 2001), 218.

16. From a sermon by Rev. George Thompson, preached on June 25, 2000, at Providence United Methodist Church, online at *www.providenceumc .org/sermons/s_000625.htm.*

17. Donald W. Shriver, "Buried Truth," *Christian Century* (February 27– March 6, 2002): 38.

18. John McTiernan, quoted by Michael Fleming, "The Extreme Sport of Being John McTiernan," *Movieline* (August 2001): 63.

19. Proverbs 22:28. Everywhere else when reference is made to removing landmarks, the scriptural context clarifies that the concern is for justice to be observed toward a neighbor's property rights: "Do not remove an ancient landmark/or encroach on the field of orphans" (Prov. 23:10); "You must not remove your neighbor's boundary marker" (Deut. 19:14); "Cursed be anyone who moves a neighbor's boundary marker" (Deut. 27:17). If these passages are interpreted as metaphors for the way we are to treat other people, they would support respect for others' gender identities and personal gender presentations, not a refusal to allow for any deviation from an abstract, arbitrary norm.

20. Paraphrased from an advertising flyer produced by *The Christian Century* (Summer 2001).

21. Bishop Kenneth Carder, from a speech given at Celebrate III, a Methodist retreat held in Asheville, North Carolina, in December 1999.

Chapter 3: Virginia Ramey Mollenkott's Gender-Variant Journey

1. Judge Roy Moore, as quoted by Mel White and Gary Nixon, *Soulforce* newsletter, May 1, 2002.

2. Anyone who doubts that male primacy is still in place should read Deborah L. Rhode, *Speaking of Sex: The Denial of Gender Inequality* (Cambridge, Mass.: Harvard University Press, 1997).

3. Jesus spoke well of eunuchs in Matthew 19, the closest the New Testament comes to explicit mention of transgenderists or homosexuals. See Virginia R. Mollenkott, *Omnigender: A Trans-Religious Approach* (Cleveland: Pilgrim Press, 2001), 118–20.

4. These arguments are summarized in appendix A of Virginia R. Mollenkott, *Sensuous Spirituality: Out from Fundamentalism* (New York: Crossroad, 1992), 189–93.

5. Now the Evangelical and Ecumenical Women's Caucus. For information see *www.eewc.com,* or e-mail *office@eewc.com,* or phone 316-269-9431. EEWC is inclusive and GLBT-friendly.

6. Riki Wilchins, "Airport Insecurity," *The Advocate* (June 25, 2002): 136.

7. For a good, brief explanation of why easy distinctions of *sex* as biological and *gender* as cultural do not really work, see Edward Stein, *The Mismeasure of Desire: The Science, Theory, and Ethics of Sexual Orientation* (Cambridge, Mass.: Harvard University Press, 1999), 31–38. For a much fuller explanation, see Anne Fausto-Sterling, *Sexing the Body: Gender Politics and the Construction of Sexuality* (New York: Basic Books, 2000).

8. For details concerning each of the "never minds," see *Omnigender,* 90–95, 105–7, 112.

9. See Virginia Mollenkott, *The Divine Feminine: Biblical Imagery of God as Female* (New York: Crossroad, 1983).

10. Sir Paul Harvey, *The Oxford Companion to Classical Literature* (New York: Oxford, 1986), 166.

11. Tom Hanks, *The Subversive Gospel* (Cleveland: Pilgrim Press, 2000), 182; Randy P. Conner et al., *Cassell's Encyclopedia of Queer Myth, Symbol, and Spirit* (New York: Cassell, 1997), 131–32; William A. Percy, *Pederasty and Pedagogy in Archaic Greece* (Urbana: University of Illinois Press, 1996), 63, 175–76, 179; E. R. Dodds, in *The Greeks and the Irrational* (Berkeley: University of California Press, 1951), stated that Cretan sages were influenced by Scythian shamanism, which included cross-dressing, transgenderism, and adult-adult homosexuality.

12. For discussion of Abraham, Sarah, Joseph, David and Jonathan, Ruth and Naomi, Jesus as virgin-born, eunuchs, the centurion and his boy (*pais*), and transgender imagery in the Hebrew and Christian Scriptures, see Mollenkott, *Omnigender,* 88–114.

13. Pat Conover, *Transgendered Good News* (Silver Spring, Md.: New Wineskins Press, 2002), 192, 264.

Chapter 4: Vanessa Sheridan's Gender-Variant Journey

1. Rev. David Horton, "Introduction: A Christian Response to the Cross-dresser and Transsexual," in *By the Grace of God,* ed. Julie Ann Johnson (Wheaton, Ill.: SSP Publications, 2001), 34.

2. Rita Nakashima Brock, *Journeys by Heart: A Christology of Erotic Power* (New York: Crossroad, 1998), 54.

3. Leyla Kokmen, "Body vs. Soul," in *City Pages* (Minneapolis: City Pages Media, July 17, 2002), 15.

4. Chuck Lofy, *A Grain of Wheat: Giving Voice to the Spirit of Change* (Burnsville, Minn.: Prince of Peace Publishing, 1993), 52.

5. Oswald Chambers, *The Psychology of Redemption* (London: Marshall, Morgan & Scott, 1955).

6. A unique, moving, and empowering historical perspective on this fascinating subject is available in Leslie Feinberg's book *Transgender Warriors: Making History from Joan of Arc to RuPaul* (Boston: Beacon Press, 1996).

7. Thank you, Martha Postlethwaite, chaplain of United Theological Seminary of the Twin Cities and nonjudgmental friend. Some years after you made that statement on a rainy Saturday in Minnesota, it still carries the solid ring of truth. I hope you know that you were speaking directly to my spirit on that day, and your words of wisdom continue to make a powerful difference in my life (Vanessa Sheridan).

Chapter 5: What Does It Mean to Walk a Transgender Christian Pathway?

1. Catherine Mowry LaCugna, *God for Us: The Trinity and Christian Life* (San Francisco: HarperSanFrancisco, 1991), 274.

2. Christine M. Smith, *Risking the Terror: Resurrection in This Life* (Cleveland: Pilgrim Press, 2001), 25.

3. Jack Trout and Steve Rivkin, *The New Positioning* (New York: McGraw-Hill, 1996), 14.

4. Steve Allen, *Vulgarians at the Gate* (Amherst, N.Y.: Prometheus Books, 2001), 70.

5. LaCugna, *God for Us,* 289–90.

6. Chris Swingle, "Their True Selves: Three People Find Serenity in the Decision to Change Their Gender," *Rochester Democrat and Chronicle,* October 24, 2002, 1C, 4C.

7. Michael Kimmel, *The Gendered Society* (New York: Oxford University Press, 2000), as quoted in *Publisher's Weekly,* February 21, 2000, 79. Emphasis ours.

8. Allen, *Vulgarians at the Gate,* 344.

9. Mary E. Hunt, "We Weren't Saved by a State Execution — An Interview with Rita Nakashima Brock and Rebecca Ann Parker," *Witness* 85 (April 2002): 14.

10. Ibid.

11. John W. Gardner, *The Recovery of Confidence* (New York: W. W. Norton, 1970), 29.

12. As quoted in an undated letter to NGLTF members by Lorri L. Jean, executive director of the National Gay and Lesbian Task Force, Washington, D.C.; received April 4, 2002.

13. Mark Berkson, "Belief That Other Faiths Go to Hell Leaves Little Room for Dialogue," *Minneapolis Star Tribune,* January 12, 2001, A17.

14. Carter Heyward, *Saving Jesus from Those Who Are Right* (Minneapolis: Augsburg Fortress, 1999), 9.

15. Anne Eggebroten, "Some Thoughts on the Yates Tragedy," Evangelical and Ecumenical Women's Caucus *Update* 25 (January–March 2002): 9–12.

16. Chuck Lofy, *A Grain of Wheat: Giving Voice to the Spirit of Change* (Burnsville, Minn.: Prince of Peace Publishing, 1993), 52.

17. Dann Hazel, *Witness: Gay and Lesbian Clergy Report from the Front* (Louisville: Westminster John Knox Press, 2000), 7.

18. Allen, *Vulgarians at the Gate*, 137.

19. Hazel, *Witness*, 7.

20. Robert Allen Warrior, a Native American scholar, wrote a remarkable essay called "Canaanites, Cowboys, and Indians," published in *Christianity and Crisis*, September 11, 1989. This article may be read online at *www.religion-online.org/cgi-bin/relsearchd.dll/showarticle?item_id=444*. In his treatise Warrior compares the conquest of Canaan to the similar conquest and destruction of indigenous cultures in North America. Warrior's essay is a powerful example of viewing history with fresh eyes, something to which we can all aspire.

21. Danna Nolan Fewell, "Joshua," in *Women's Bible Commentary*, ed. Carol A. Newsom and Sharon H. Ringe (Louisville: Westminster John Knox Press, 1998), 69.

22. William B. Nelson Jr., "Promised Land," in *The Oxford Companion to the Bible*, ed. Bruce M. Metzger and Michael D. Coogan (New York: Oxford University Press, 1993), 620.

23. Karen Armstrong, *The Battle for God* (New York: Ballantine Books, 2000), 321–22.

24. Smith, *Risking the Terror*, 81.

25. John Shelby Spong, *The Bishop's Voice: Selected Essays 1979–1999* (New York: Crossroad, 1999), 61.

26. Ibid., 86.

27. J. Philip Wogaman, "The Virtue of Moral Compromise," *Zion's Herald* 177 (January–February 2003): 21–22.

Chapter 6: Reclaiming Our Territory, Mapping Our Pathway

1. We use "kin-dom" rather than "kingdom" to emphasize the familiar intimacy of God's compassion and loving kindness, and to avoid suggestions of royal hierarchy and class distinctions.

2. Fred Craddock, "Test Run," *Christian Century* (February 22, 2003): 21.

3. Adapted in part and paraphrased from Vivian Jenkins Nelsen, *Diversity Dictionary: A Dictionary of Nondiscriminatory Language* (Minneapolis: Hypatia Trust, 1997), 50.

4. Karen Armstrong, *The Battle for God* (New York: Ballantine Books, 2000), 135.

5. Ibid., 140.

6. Ibid., 270.

7. Chuck Lofy, *A Grain of Wheat: Giving Voice to the Spirit of Change* (Burnsville, Minn.: Prince of Peace Publishing, 1993), 35.

8. Ibid., 41.

9. Ibid., 35–36.

10. Ibid., 39.

11. Christine M. Smith, *Risking the Terror: Resurrection in This Life* (Cleveland: Pilgrim Press, 2001), 13.

12. Lofy, *A Grain of Wheat*, 41.

13. Katherine Kersten, "Many Are Hurt by the Laissez-Faire Family," *Minneapolis Star Tribune*, July 25, 2001, A19.

14. His Holiness the Dalai Lama and Howard C. Cutler, M.D., *The Art of Happiness: A Handbook for Living* (New York: Penguin Putnam, 1998), 31.

15. Jack Trout and Steve Rivkin, *The New Positioning* (New York: McGraw-Hill, 1996), 12.

16. Arlene Stein, *The Stranger Next Door: The Story of a Small Community's Battle over Sex, Faith, and Civil Rights* (Boston: Beacon Press, 2001), 127.

17. Michael J. Mazza, "Texts of Terror, Texts of Hope: Teaching the Bible as Literature in a Gay-Friendly Context," online at *www.whosoever.org/v4i3/mazza.html*.

18. Stein, *The Stranger Next Door*, 8.

19. Ibid.

20. Kai Erickson, *Wayward Puritans: A Study in the Sociology of Deviance* (New York: John Wiley and Sons, 1966), 8–19.

21. Robert Scott and Jack Douglas, *Theoretical Perspectives on Deviance* (New York: Basic Books, 1972), 29.

22. Stein, *The Stranger Next Door*, 8.

23. From welcoming remarks by Rev. Rebecca Voelkel of Spirit of the Lakes United Church of Christ, Minneapolis, for a Community Forum and Conversation held on December 12, 2001.

24. Smith, *Risking the Terror*, 83.

25. Nancy Crowe, *Bethlehem Road* (Anaheim, Calif.: Odd Girls Press, 2002).

26. As quoted in *Soaring with Wingspan Newsletter*, May 20, 2001, 1.

27. From a sermon by Rev. Anita C. Hill, preached on May 6, 2001, at St. Paul-Reformation Church, St. Paul, Minn., quoted in *Soaring with Wingspan Newsletter*, May 20, 2001, 3.

28. John Shelby Spong, *The Bishop's Voice: Selected Essays 1979–1999* (New York: Crossroad, 1999), xvi.

Chapter 7: Developing a Theology for the Transgender Journey

1. Christine E. Gudorf, "The Erosion of Sexual Dimorphism: Challenges to Religion and Religious Ethics," *Journal of the American Academy of Religion* 69 (December 2001): 874.

2. Ibid., 871. Although we have added gender to Professor Gudorf's statement, our addition is in line with the overall tenor of her article. She points out that "it is no longer correct to distinguish sex and gender by saying that sex refers to our biological givenness as male or female and gender refers to the traits and roles that a particular society and individuals construct for male and female persons. Today we should recognize that both sex and gender are socially constructed categories; both sex and gender must be interpreted" (876).

3. Lacey Leigh, *Out and About: The Emancipated Crossdresser* (Phoenix: Double Star Press, 2001), 55.

4. David Hansen, *A Little Handbook on Having a Soul* (Downers Grove, Ill.: InterVarsity Press, 1997).

5. Karen Armstrong, *The Battle for God* (New York: Ballantine Books, 2000), xi.

6. Ibid., 204.

7. Chuck Lofy, *A Grain of Wheat: Giving Voice to the Spirit of Change* (Burnsville, Minn.: Prince of Peace Publishing, 1993), 37–38.

8. Peter Gomes, *The Good Book: Reading the Bible with Mind and Heart* (New York: Avon Books, 1996), 116.

9. Grant R. Osborne, *The Hermeneutical Spiral: A Comprehensive Introduction to Biblical Interpretation* (Downers Grove, Ill.: InterVarsity Press, 1991), 405.

10. Arthur Miller's play *The Crucible,* set in seventeenth-century Massachusetts during the period of the witch-hunts, is an example of the toxic and even lethal consequences that can result when such a closed, rigid socioreligious mind-set is permitted to dominate a community. The 1978 suicide cult horror of Jim Jones and the People's Temple in Guyana is perhaps a more recent reminder of what can happen when false religion is undeterred by reason and right relationship.

11. Gomes, *The Good Book,* 116.

12. John Shelby Spong, *The Bishop's Voice: Selected Essays 1979–1999* (New York: Crossroad, 1999), 120.

13. Archibald A. Hodge and Benjamin Warfield, "Inspiration," *Princeton Review* 2 (April 11, 1881).

14. Armstrong, *The Battle for God,* 141–42.

15. Ibid., 142.

16. Gomes, *The Good Book,* 45.

17. Ibid.

18. Ibid.

19. Among those engaging in this selective literalism are Ed Wheat, *Problems and Sex Techniques in Marriage* (Springdale, Ariz.: Bible Believers Cassettes, 1975); Herbert J. Miles, *Sexual Happiness in Marriage* (Grand Rapids, Mich.: Zondervan, 1967), 81; and Tim and Beverly LaHaye, *The Act of Marriage* (Grand Rapids, Mich.: Zondervan, 1976), 275. See Letha Dawson Scanzoni and Virginia Ramey Mollenkott, *Is the Homosexual My Neighbor?* rev. and updated (San Francisco: HarperSanFrancisco, 1994), 132–34.

20. L. William Countryman, *Dirt, Greed, and Sex: Sexual Ethics in the New Testament and Their Implications for Today* (Philadelphia: Fortress Press, 1988), 26–27.

21. Judith Romney Wagner, "Leviticus," in *Women's Bible Commentary,* expanded ed., ed. Carol A. Newsom and Sharon H. Ringe (Louisville: Westminster John Knox Press, 1998), 43.

22. Vern L. Bullough and Bonnie Bullough, *Cross Dressing, Sex, and Gender* (Philadelphia: University of Pennsylvania Press, 1993), 39–40. The Bulloughs point out that cross-dressing in Israel was far more frequent than Deuteronomy 22:5 would indicate, including cross-dressing at festivals and events carried out on stage.

23. Leigh, *Out and About,* 55.

24. Rembert S. Truluck, *Steps to Recovery from Bible Abuse* (Gaithersburg, Md.: Chi Rho Press, 2000), 20.

25. Stephen Denning, *The Springboard: How Storytelling Ignites Action in Knowledge-Era Organizations* (Woburn, Mass.: Butterworth-Heineman, 2001), 71.

Chapter 8: Coming Out As an Act of Faith

1. Christine M. Smith, *Risking the Terror: Resurrection in This Life* (Cleveland: Pilgrim Press, 2001), 94.

2. Lee Frances Heller, "The Dew of Grace," in *By the Grace of God,* ed. Julie Ann Johnson (Wheaton, Ill.: SSP Publications, 2001), 153.

3. Ibid.

4. Emilie M. Townes, "Ethics As an Art of Doing the Work Our Souls Must Have," in *The Arts of Ministry: Feminist-Womanist Approaches,* ed. Christie Cozad Neuger (Louisville: Westminster John Knox Press, 1996), 157.

5. See the statement at *www.amazon.com/exec/obidos/tg/guides/guide -display/-/223QTZJ3DSFQX/ref=cm_bg_dp_l_1/002-4418765-3524018.*

6. Rev. Dr. William R. Johnson, "Protestantism and Gay and Lesbian Freedom," in *Positively Gay: New Approaches to Gay and Lesbian Life* (Berkeley, Calif.: Celestial Arts, 2001), 218.

7. E. D. Hirsch Jr., Joseph F. Kett, James Trefil, *The Dictionary of Cultural Literacy* (Boston: Houghton Mifflin, 1993), 284–85.

8. James Melvin Washington, *A Testament of Hope: The Essential Writings of Martin Luther King, Jr.* (San Francisco: Harper & Row, 1986), 292–93.

9. Pat Conover, *Transgender Good News* (Silver Spring, Md.: New Wineskin Press, 2002), 125–29.

10. Lacey Leigh, *Out and About: The Emancipated Crossdresser* (Phoenix: Double Star Press, 2001), 14.

11. Betty Berzon, *Positively Gay: New Approaches to Gay and Lesbian Life* (Berkeley, Calif.: Celestial Arts, 2001), 27.

12. Mildred L. Brown and Chloe Ann Rounsley, *True Selves: Understanding Transsexualism* (San Francisco: Jossey Bass, 1996), 162–66.

13. Dann Hazel, *Witness: Gay and Lesbian Clergy Report from the Front* (Louisville: Westminster John Knox Press, 2000), 3.

14. Fritz Klein and Thomas Schwartz, eds., *Bisexual and Gay Husbands: Their Stories, Their Words* (New York: Harrington Park Press, 2001), 61–62.

15. Jamal Badawi, as quoted by Diana L. Eck in *A New Religious America: How a "Christian Country" Has Become the World's Most Religiously Diverse Nation* (New York: HarperSanFrancisco, 2001), 238.

16. Leigh, *Out and About,* 14.

17. IFGE is the world's largest transgender-based organization, with education, outreach, and research efforts being conducted on an ongoing basis. Contact them at *IFGE@world.std.com* or by mail at IFGE, P.O. Box 229, Waltham, MA 02154. Their phone number is 617-894-8340.

18. The UCC's Coalition can be reached online at *www.ucccoalition.org,* by mail at UCC Coalition for LGBT Concerns, PMB 230, 800 Village Walk, Guilford, CT 06437, or by phone at 800-653-0799.

19. Contact PFLAG by phone at 202-467-8181; by mail at 1726 M Street, NW, Suite 400, Washington, DC 20000, or log onto *www.pflag.org.*

20. Youtha Hardman-Cromwell, "Spirituality and Sexuality: Both or Neither," in *Shaping Sanctuary,* ed. Kelly Turney (Chicago: Reconciling Congregation Program, 2000), 8.

21. Peter Gomes, *The Good Book: Reading the Bible with Mind and Heart* (New York: Avon Books, 1996), 118.

22. Marianne Williamson, *A Return to Love: Reflections on the Principles of a Course in Miracles* (New York: Harper Collins, 1992), chapter 7, sec. 3.

23. Berzon, *Positively Gay,* 18–19.

24. Ibid.

25. From "Domestic Partner Benefits for All," *Lavender,* Lavender Media, Minneapolis, 7, no. 180, 8.

26. Leigh, *Out and About,* 24.

27. Michael "Miqqui Alicia" Gilbert, *The Transgendered Philosopher,* online at *www.symposion.com/ijt/gilbert/gilbert.htm.*

28. Rembert S. Truluck, *Steps to Recovery from Bible Abuse* (Gaithersburg, Md.: Chi Rho Press, 2000), 27–28.

29. Townes, "Ethics As an Art of Doing the Work Our Souls Must Have," 149.

Chapter 9: Wilderness Pilgrims and Prophets

1. Delores S. Williams, *Sisters in the Wilderness: The Challenge of Womanist God-Talk* (Maryknoll, N.Y.: Orbis Books, 1993), 15, 33.

2. Ibid., 23.

3. Ibid., 32.

4. See John 4:44.

5. Tom Hanks, *The Subversive Gospel: A New Testament Commentary of Liberation* (Cleveland: Pilgrim Press, 2000), 182. See also *Cassell's Encyclopedia of Queer Myth, Symbol, and Spirit* (New York: Cassell, 1998), 131–32.

6. Kathleen D. Billman, "Pastoral Care As an Art of Community," in *The Arts of Ministry: Feminist-Womanist Approaches,* ed. Christie Cozad Neuger (Louisville: Westminster John Knox Press, 1996), 30.

7. See Virginia Ramey Mollenkott, *The Divine Feminine: The Biblical Imagery of God as Female* (New York: Crossroad, 1983), esp. 108–9.

8. Christie Cozad Neuger, "Pastoral Counseling As an Art of Personal Political Activism," in *The Arts of Ministry: Feminist-Womanist Approaches,* ed. Christie Cozad Neuger (Louisville: Westminster John Knox Press, 1996), 95.

9. Mary Ballou and Nancy Gabalac, *A Feminist Position on Mental Health* (Springfield, Ill.: Thomas Press, 1985), chap. 4.

10. Neuger, "Pastoral Counseling As an Art of Personal Political Activism," 111.

11. Ibid., 113.

12. John Shelby Spong, *A New Christianity for a New World: Why Traditional Faith Is Dying and How a New Faith Is Being Born* (New York: HarperSanFrancisco, 2001), x.

13. For more about the overt transgender aspects of the Christian church, see Vanessa Sheridan, *Crossing Over: Liberating the Transgendered Christian* (Cleveland: Pilgrim Press, 2001), esp. chap. 7.

Chapter 10: Steps That Lie Ahead

1. Online at *www.geocities.com/Athens/Acropolis/3345/austral.html.*

2. It is not our intention to denigrate the work that many caring professional researchers, counselors, psychiatrists, psychologists, and others do in concert with the transgender community. Our purpose is, instead, to assist in the struggle to remove the ultimate responsibility for gender-variant lives from the hands of the academy and from mental health professionals. We transgender people need to take on that responsibility for ourselves. We cannot continue allowing others to define or control the circumstances of our lives; we are not puppets or incapacitated simply because we are transgender. Gender-variant persons need to pursue and demand autonomy rather than continue operating from a paradigm of dependency upon professionals, no matter how well-intentioned those professionals may be.

3. Handt Hanson, *Mission-Driven Worship: Helping Your Changing Church Celebrate God* (Burnsville, Minn.: Changing Church Forum, 2001), 40.

4. Terri Main, "For They Know Not What They Do," in *By the Grace of God,* ed. Julie Ann Johnson (Wheaton, Ill.: SSP Publications, 2001), 297–98.

5. Ibid.

6. See James A. Doyle, *Sex and Gender* (Dubuque, Iowa: William C. Brown, 1985).

7. Carol Lakey Hess, "Education As an Art of Getting Dirty with Dignity," in *The Arts of Ministry: Feminist-Womanist Approaches,* ed. Christie Cozad Neuger (Louisville: Westminster John Knox Press, 1996), 61.

8. William Wordsworth, *Ode: Intimations of Immortality from Recollections of Early Childhood (1802–4).*

9. Susan Faludi, *Stiffed: The Betrayal of the American Man* (New York: Wm. Morrow, 1999), 14–15.

10. Ibid., 263.

11. Ibid., 265.

12. Pat Conover, *Transgender Good News* (Silver Spring, Md.: New Wineskin Press, 2002), 82.

13. Marcus J. Borg, *Jesus: A New Vision* (San Francisco: HarperSanFrancisco, 1987), 82.

14. Catherine Mowry LaCugna, *God with Us: The Trinity and Christian Life* (San Francisco: HarperSanFrancisco, 1991), 15.

15. Ibid.

16. Walter Brueggemann, *The Bible Makes Sense* (Louisville: Westminster John Knox Press, 2001), 79.

17. Posted on the Internet by permission of the author, the Reverend Canon Jay D. Wegman. Copyright 2000. Personal communication to V. R. Mollenkott from C. A. Bradley, June 29, 2002.

18. Ganymede was the cup-bearer and boy beloved by Zeus. In the Renaissance, "Ganymede" was a code word for a male beloved by another male.

19. Robert E. Goss, *Queering Christ: Beyond Jesus Acted Up* (Cleveland: Pilgrim Press, 2002), 128, 130–31, 49, 125, 180, 164–65.

20. See Virginia R. Mollenkott, *Omnigender: A Trans-Religious Approach* (Cleveland: Pilgrim Press, 2001), 105–7.

21. See Vanessa Sheridan, *Crossing Over: Liberating the Transgendered Christian* (Cleveland: Pilgrim Press, 2001), chap. 7, esp. 93–107.

22. From "Joy, Dancing, and Wisdom Greater Than Despair," a sermon by Rev. Rebecca Voelkel, preached on July 14, 2002, at Spirit of the Lakes United Church of Christ, Minneapolis.